# ESSENTIAL APPROACH FOR THE TOEIC® L&R TEST
## − Revised Edition −

TOEIC® L&R TESTへのニューアプローチ

Naoko Osuka
Hisakazu Tsukano
Atsuko Yamamoto
Robert Van Benthuysen

写真提供
大須賀 直子
塚野 壽一
山本 厚子
毎日新聞社情報サービスセンター
iStock
pixta

### 音声ファイルのダウンロード／ストリーミング

CDマーク表示がある箇所は、音声を弊社HPより無料でダウンロード／ストリーミングすることができます。トップページのバナーをクリックし、書籍検索してください。書籍詳細ページに音声ダウンロードアイコンがございますのでそちらから自習用音声としてご活用ください。

https://www.seibido.co.jp

### ESSENTIAL APPROACH FOR THE TOEIC® L&R TEST

Copyright © 2019 by Naoko Osuka, Hisakazu Tsukano,
Atsuko Yamamoto, Robert Van Benthuysen

*All rights reserved for Japan*
*No part of this book may be reproduced in any form*
*without permission from Seibido Co., Ltd.*

# は し が き

　本書の前作である "Essential Approach for the TOEIC® Test" が発行されてから10年が経ちました。その間、科学技術の発達はめざましく、経済・金融にも大きな影響を与え、ビジネスのやり方も変わってきました。また、社会、経済のグローバル化がますます進み、国際的共通語としての英語を使えることの重要性はさらに高まっています。

　こうした状況の中で、2016年5月にTOEICテストの形式が10年ぶりに一部変更されました。この変更は、「TOEICテストには日々変化する英語の使い方、そして日常やビジネスでの英語によるコミュニケーション方法が反映される」という考えに基づいています。リスニング問題には、3人の会話問題や図表・地図などを含む問題が加わり、gonna や wanna などの口語的表現が一部に使われるようになりました。リーディング問題には、オンラインのチャット問題や3つの関連する文書を読んで答える Triple Passages の問題が加わりました。全体的には、英文の量や複雑性が増して、難易度は確実に上がったと言えるでしょう。

　このような TOEIC テストの変更に対応すべく、前作を改訂して出来上がったのが本書です。新形式に対応して、上記のような変更点はすべて問題に組み入れました。また、前作の長所を残すとともに、この10年間で大きく変わったビジネス・コミュニケーションのやり方を反映させて、現代に合った内容に作り変えました。

　本書の特長は、ユニットごとに、特定のテーマのもとに Part 1 から Part 7 がすべて含まれていて使いやすいこと、リスニング・スキルや文法について各ユニットで説明がなされ、問題練習を通じて段階的に習得できること、さらには語彙や連語の重要性を踏まえ、様々なタイプの語彙練習問題が含まれていることなどです。また、毎ユニットに「TOEIC テスト攻略のコツ」を掲載しましたので、是非ご参照ください。初中級レベルの大学生が TOEIC テストで高得点を取るための実践力をつけるばかりではなく、より広い意味での聴解力、文法力、語彙力、読解力も伸ばせるような構成となっています。

　本テキストを通じて、学習者が TOEIC テストで高得点を取れるとともに、総合的な英語能力を伸ばせるように心より願っております。

2018年　秋

# 本テキストの構成と使い方

**Vocabulary**  基本語彙2,000語を超えるものを中心に選んだ15の語句は、すべて各ユニットの練習問題で使用されています。英語はアルファベット順、日本語はあいうえお順に配列されています。音声を聴いて発音もチェックしましょう。

**Word Pairs**  各ユニットのテーマに関連する熟語や、使用頻度の高いコロケーション（連語）を取り上げました。ペアで覚えましょう。

**Listening Skill**  英語の聴解力アップにつながる、基本的なリスニング・スキルについて、簡略に解説しています。例題も付いていますので、実際に問題を解いて身につけましょう。

**TOEIC Parts 1~7**  新形式問題に対応し、各パートの問題数の比率が実際の TOEIC テストの問題とほぼ同じになるように配列されています。リスニング問題では、アメリカ英語に加えてイギリス英語、カナダ英語、オーストラリア英語など多様な英語も取り上げています。 各ユニットの Parts 1〜7の正解率が70％（全24問中17問）以上になるように頑張りましょう。

**TOEIC攻略のコツ**  TOEIC テスト Parts 1〜7の問題を解くためのコツを取り上げました。リスニングセクションでは、3人の会話問題、図表を含めた会話や説明文問題など、リーディングセクションでは、チャット形式の問題、3つの文書を読んで解答する問題などの新しい出題形式が加わりました。TOEIC攻略のコツを読んで、TOEIC テストの全体像を把握しましょう。

**文法問題攻略のポイント**  ユニット別に、TOEIC テストに頻出する文法項目について説明しています。また各ユニットの Parts 5〜6には、その章の文法項目を含む問題が必ず含まれていますので、確実に習得するように努めましょう。

**Expand your vocabulary!**  語彙を増やす方法を習得するためのコーナーです。接尾辞、接頭辞、派生語などを活用して、語彙を増やしましょう。

**Learn More! – Vocabulary in Context**  このセクションでは、各ユニットのテーマに関連した重要語彙を問題形式で提示しています。問題を解いて重要語彙を習得しましょう。

**Scoreboard**  ユニットごとに得点を記入するようになっています。特にできなかったユニットの文法や語彙はしっかり復習しましょう。

**Vocabulary List**  「Vocabulary」、「Word Pairs」、「Learn more! – Vocabulary in Context」で取り上げられた語句がアルファベット順に並んでいます。復習に役立てましょう。

# CONTENTS

**1 Arts & Amusement** ............. 6
芸術と娯楽
◆音の変化に気をつけよう(1)[音の脱落]
■名詞&代名詞

**2 Lunch & Parties** ................... 15
ランチとパーティー
◆音の変化に気をつけよう(2)[子音と母音の連結①]
■形容詞&冠詞

**3 Medicine & Health** .............. 24
医療と健康
◆音の変化に気をつけよう(3)[子音と母音の連結②]
■副詞

**4 Traffic & Travel** ................... 33
交通と旅行
◆音の変化に気をつけよう(4)[音の混合]
■比較

**5 Ordering & Shipping** ......... 42
注文と輸送
◆音の変化に気をつけよう(5)[t 音の変化]
■動詞&時制

**6 Factories & Production** ... 51
工場と製造
◆いろいろな数字に慣れよう！
■未来表現など

**7 Research & Development** ...60
研究と開発
◆英語とカタカナ表記との発音の違いを認識しよう。
■主語と動詞の呼応、時制の一致

**8 Computers & Technology** ... 69
コンピュータと科学技術
◆トピックが何なのかを把握しよう！
■能動態&受動態

**9 Employment & Promotions** .... 78
雇用と昇進
◆会話や説明文の状況・場所・人間関係を把握しよう！
■不定詞&動名詞

**10 Advertisements & Personnel** ... 87
宣伝と人事
◆場面をイメージしよう！
■分詞

**11 Telephone & Messages** ... 96
電話とメッセージ
◆英語の話の展開の特徴を知ろう
■助動詞

**12 Banking & Finance** ........... 105
銀行業務と財務
◆すべての語句を聞きとろうとしない
■接続詞

**13 Office Work & Equipment** .... 115
オフィス業務と備品
◆繰り返し出てくる語句に注意しよう
■関係代名詞&関係副詞

**14 Housing & Properties** ..... 124
住宅と不動産
◆頭の中で日本語に訳さない
■前置詞

**15 Business & Management** ... 133
ビジネスと経営
◆最後まで集中力を持続させよう
■条件文など

Scoreboard ..................... 142
Vocabulary List ............. 143

*******
◆…Listening Skill
■…文法問題攻略のポイント

# Unit 1

## Arts & Amusement

このユニットでは、芸術や娯楽についてのトピックを扱います。私たちの生活に潤いと喜びを与えてくれるこれらのトピックが、TOEIC テストではどのように出題されるのかを見てみましょう。

## ■ Vocabulary *Match each English word with its meaning in Japanese.* 1-02

| | | |
|---|---|---|
| 1. abide by ( ) | 2. accustomed ( ) | 3. costume ( ) |
| 4. discourage ( ) | 5. exhibit ( ) | 6. fee ( ) |
| 7. graduate ( ) | 8. install ( ) | 9. landscape ( ) |
| 10. leisurely ( ) | 11. prohibit ( ) | 12. reputation ( ) |
| 13. sculpture ( ) | 14. thrilling ( ) | 15. worthwhile ( ) |

a. 衣装　　b. 禁止する　　c. 設置する　　d. 卒業する・卒業生　　e. 彫刻
f. 展示（する）　　g. 慣れた　　h. 評判　　i. 風景　　j. 守る　　k. やめるよう説得する
l. やりがいのある　　m. ゆったりした　　n. 料金　　o. わくわくさせる

## ■ Word Pairs *Fill in each blank to complete the sentences.*

1. Science fiction movies often use (　　　　　)(　　　　　).

2. She was (　　　　　)(　　　　　) the best actress award.

3. Every student at this school is required to play at least one (　　　　　)
(　　　　　).

4. The (　　　　　)(　　　　　) the orchestra.

5. That (　　　　　)(　　　　　) is popular among families with young children.

| | | |
|---|---|---|
| a. nominated / for | b. musical / instrument | c. special / effects |
| d. amusement / park | e. audience / applauded | |

# Listening

## Listening Skill：音の変化に気をつけよう⑴　［音の脱落］

英語が話されるとき、単語が1語ずつ発音記号と同じように発音されるわけではなく、様々な音の変化が起こります。たとえば、単語の一部の音がほとんど聞こえないことがよくあります。文中の［h］音や語尾の［t］、［p］音などは脱落しやすいので気をつけましょう。（例：I asked him to get the ticket.）

## Example 🎧1-03

*You'll see a picture and hear four short statements. Fill in the blanks and choose the statement that best describes what you see in the picture.*

(A) The man is looking (　　)(　　) picture.

(B) The man is putting (　　)(　　) picture.

(C) The man is taking a picture.

(D) The man is talking (　　)(　　) picture.

Ⓐ Ⓑ Ⓒ Ⓓ

## Part 1　Photographs

*You'll see a picture and hear four short statements. Choose the statement that best describes what you see in the picture.*

Ⓐ Ⓑ Ⓒ Ⓓ

Ⓐ Ⓑ Ⓒ Ⓓ

# Part 2 Question - Response (CD)1-06,07,08,09

*You'll hear a question followed by three responses. Choose the best response to each question.*

3. Mark your answer on your answer sheet.  Ⓐ Ⓑ Ⓒ

4. Mark your answer on your answer sheet.  Ⓐ Ⓑ Ⓒ

5. Mark your answer on your answer sheet.  Ⓐ Ⓑ Ⓒ

6. Mark your answer on your answer sheet.  Ⓐ Ⓑ Ⓒ


# Part 3 Conversation (CD)1-10,11

*You'll hear one conversation between two people and read three questions followed by four answers. Choose the best answer to each question.*

7. Where will the exhibition be held?
   (A) The Gallery of Contemporary Art
   (B) The City Arts Academy
   (C) The Third Street Gallery
   (D) The Museum of Contemporary Painting

   Ⓐ Ⓑ Ⓒ Ⓓ

8. When can the woman go to the exhibition?
   (A) This evening
   (B) Friday
   (C) Saturday
   (D) Sunday

   Ⓐ Ⓑ Ⓒ Ⓓ

9. What kind of art will they see?
   (A) Old paintings
   (B) New paintings
   (C) Contemporary sculpture
   (D) Old sculpture

   Ⓐ Ⓑ Ⓒ Ⓓ

# Part 4 Talk ◎ 1-12,13

*You'll hear one talk and read three questions about the talk. The questions will be followed by four answers. Choose the best answer to each question.*

**10.** What time will the show begin?
- (A) 1 : 30
- (B) 2 : 00
- (C) 2 : 30
- (D) 3 : 00

Ⓐ Ⓑ Ⓒ Ⓓ

**11.** Where would you hear this announcement?
- (A) At a movie theater
- (B) At a sports stadium
- (C) At a circus
- (D) At a theme park

Ⓐ Ⓑ Ⓒ Ⓓ

**12.** What does "the real stars of our show will be the unbelievable whales and dolphins of Ocean World" mean?
- (A) The whales and dolphins are not real.
- (B) The whales and dolphins are the only performers in the show.
- (C) There are no human performers in the show.
- (D) The whales and dolphins will give a great performance.

Ⓐ Ⓑ Ⓒ Ⓓ

---

## TOEIC 攻略のコツ：Parts 1-4　同じまたは似た発音の単語に注意

リスンニング問題では、flower と flour, sail と sale, steal と steel などのような同音異義語や、want と won't, staff と stuff, wash と wish などの似た発音の単語が選択肢に入っていて、まどわされることがあります。音声だけにとらわれずに、文脈から判断して正解を選べるようにしましょう。

# Reading

## 文法問題攻略のポイント：名詞＆代名詞

1. 名詞には数えられる名詞と数えられない名詞がある。数えられない名詞には、抽象名詞、物質名詞、固有名詞、一部の集合名詞があり、原則として複数形にならない。
   例1：I cannot live without **music**.（抽象名詞）
   例2：You can buy **ice cream** at a stand in the park.（物質名詞）
2. 日本人には数えられるように感じられても、英語では数えられない場合がある。
   例：Let me give you some **information** about the museum.
   この他にも、news, mail, advice, baggage [luggage], furniture, equipment などは数えられない名詞である。
3. 代名詞は、先行する名詞の数に呼応し、文中における働きに応じて格（主格・所有格・目的格）が決まる。
   例：<u>Tom and I</u> went on a picnic, and **we** had lunch on the top of the hill.
4. 目的語が主語と同じ人・物をさすときは、再帰代名詞（-self/-selves）が用いられる。
   例：<u>He</u> has an ability to express **himself** in writing.

## Part 5 Incomplete Sentences

*A word or phrase is missing in each sentence. Choose the best answer to complete the sentence.*

13. I cannot go to the movies tonight because I have ____ homework.
    (A) quite a few
    (B) many
    (C) a lot of
    (D) no

14. There was _____ audience at the band's concert.
    (A) a large
    (B) a few
    (C) many
    (D) a lot

15. I enjoyed _____ very much at the party yesterday.
    (A) my
    (B) me
    (C) mine
    (D) myself

16. I will drop Tom and Mary off at the theater, and I will pick _____ up at three o'clock.
    (A) they
    (B) them
    (C) their
    (D) theirs

# Part 6 Text Completion

*Read the following advertisement. A word, phrase, or sentence is missing. Choose the best answer to complete the text.*

*Questions 17-19 refer to the following article.*

## Holiday in Majorca

*Holiday in Majorca* is a romantic comedy starring Jane Rogers. She was nominated for an Academy Award for her attractive performance in this movie. ( **17** ) is based on the No.1 best-selling book, *Under the Sun of Majorca*. The author, Mary Turner, created the story from her own experience. New York writer Katy Lane breaks up with ( **18** ) boyfriend, and leaves for Majorca to spend two weeks there. She finds life there much slower and easier. ( **19** ). Her best friend Rachel also comes to the house and they live together, helping each other. The landscape of Majorca is also fascinating. You might want to live in Majorca like Katy.

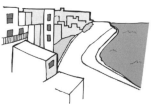

17. (A) She
    (B) He
    (C) It
    (D) What

18. (A) she
    (B) her
    (C) hers
    (D) herself

19. (A) For example, she doesn't have to worry about how to live a leisurely life.
    (B) Finally, she decides to live there and buys a small house.
    (C) However, she decides to rent a house.
    (D) Moreover, she needs to buy a house.

# Part 7 Reading Comprehension (Single Passages)

*Read the following texts. Each text or set of texts is followed by several questions. Choose the best answer to each question.*

*Questions 20-21 refer to the following notice.*

## Oceanside Aquarium Guidelines

In order that everyone can have a good time at our aquarium, we ask you to follow these guidelines.

1. Flash photography is prohibited.
2. You are not allowed to bring any food or drinks.
3. No pets are allowed.
4. It is preferable you put your large bags in the lockers.
5. Please refrain from touching the fish and sea animals except in fish-touching corners.
6. You are only allowed to smoke in a designated area on each floor.
7. The use of mobile phones is discouraged.

We hope your visit to our aquarium will be enjoyable and worthwhile by abiding by the guidelines.

20. What can you do in the aquarium?
  (A) Use your cell phone freely
  (B) Take pictures everywhere
  (C) Touch fish everywhere
  (D) Bring your dogs or cats

21. In the notice, the word "designated" in the guideline No.6 is closest in meaning to
  (A) designed
  (B) elected
  (C) installed
  (D) appointed

*Questions 22-24 refer to the following poster.*

# Richmond Art Museum

Richmond Art Museum presents Grandma Moses' special exhibition now.
Time : 10:00-17:00, May 1-June 30, closed on Mondays
Entrance fee : $ 8 for adults, $ 3 for children (4-13 yrs old), & free for children under 4
Come and appreciate her marvelous artworks!

## GRANDMA MOSES

In 1938, an art collector, Louis Caldor, was driving through the countryside of New York. He stopped at a drugstore to get a drink.

He found several paintings hung there. The artist was a 77-year-old local woman named Anna Moses, who had just recently started painting in her own style. Caldor visited Moses' home to see more of her paintings and was very impressed.

Thanks to Caldor's efforts, Moses' paintings were soon exhibited at the Museum of Modern Art. The show was a great success.

After that, Moses painted for almost 25 more years. She always painted what she saw and what she remembered — the people and scenes of the New England countryside. People found her paintings attractive and she became known as Grandma Moses. She became one of the most loved folk artists of the 20th century.

22. How did Caldor find Moses' paintings?
    (A) An owner of a drugstore recommended her paintings to him.
    (B) He heard of her reputation and visited her.
    (C) He saw her paintings by accident.
    (D) Moses visited him and showed her paintings.

23. Why was Anna Moses called "Grandma Moses"?
    (A) She was a grandmother of a famous person.
    (B) She painted pictures for a long time.
    (C) She became famous after she got old.
    (D) She painted her grandmother.

**24.** What is NOT true about Grandma Moses?
  (A) She painted scenes from her own country life.
  (B) She taught herself how to paint.
  (C) She became famous in a short while.
  (D) She painted abstract pictures.

Ⓐ Ⓑ Ⓒ Ⓓ

# Expand your vocabulary! —接尾辞で品詞がわかる！【名詞】

➤ **-ment** （例：amusement, entertainment）
➤ **-ance, -ence** （例：performance, audience）
➤ **-age** （例：marriage, average）
➤ **-th** （例：length, growth）
➤ **-ness** （例：happiness, kindness）
➤ **-tion, -sion** （例：attraction, admission）
➤ **-ty, -cy** （例：popularity, emergency）

# Learn more! — Vocabulary in Context

*Complete each English sentence according to its Japanese translation. The first letter is given.*

1. The audience did not stop (c          ) their hands in appreciation of the (c      ).
   （作曲家を賞賛して、聴衆の拍手は鳴り止まなかった。）

2. The author displayed his outstanding talent in his new (n         ), which strongly appealed to (c      ).
   （その作家は新しい小説で傑出した才能を示し、それは批評家に強くアピールした。）

3. The movie was boring, and I was (d       ) with the (d      ).
   （その映画は退屈で、私は監督にがっかりした。）

4. The whole audience (h       ) their (b      ), waiting to see what the actor would do next in the scene.
   （観客全員がかたずをのんで、その演劇で役者が次に何をするかを見守っていた。）

1. clapping, composer  2. novel, critics  3. disappointed, director  4. held, breath

# Unit 2

## Lunch & Parties

TOEIC テストでは、ビジネスシーンからだけでなく、ランチ、ディナー、パーティなどを扱った問題も出題されます。食に関する基本的な英語表現や単語をしっかり覚えておきましょう。

■ **Vocabulary** *Match each English word with its meaning in Japanese.* 🎧1-14

| | | | | | |
|---|---|---|---|---|---|
| 1. aboard ( ) | 2. buffet ( ) | 3. colleague ( ) |
| 4. crew ( ) | 5. diner ( ) | 6. dissolve ( ) |
| 7. fabulous ( ) | 8. ingredient ( ) | 9. intake ( ) |
| 10. luncheon ( ) | 11. mash ( ) | 12. moderate ( ) |
| 13. patron ( ) | 14. recipe ( ) | 15. ripe ( ) |

**a.** 熟れた　　**b.** 簡易食堂　　**c.**（ひいき）客　　**d.**（料理の）材料　　**e.** 素晴らしい
**f.** すりつぶす　　**g.**（食品などの）摂取　　**h.** 昼食会　　**i.** 調理法　　**j.** 適度の
**k.** 搭乗して　　**l.** 同僚　　**m.** 溶かす　　**n.** ビュッフェ　　**o.** 乗組員

■ **Word Pairs** *Fill in each blank to complete the sentences.*

1. Please (　　　　　) a (　　　　　　) for two people at 5：00 next Friday.

2. If you have a coupon, you can have a soft drink (　　　　　)(　　　　　　).

3. I (　　　　　) a good (　　　　　　) talking with people at the party.

4. You can choose from a (　　　　　)(　　　　　　) of foods.

5. Would you (　　　　　)(　　　　　　) another cup of coffee?

| | | |
|---|---|---|
| **a.** care / for | **b.** make / reservation | **c.** for / free |
| **d.** wide / variety | **e.** had / time | |

# Listening

## Listening Skill：音の変化に気をつけよう⑵　[子音と母音の連結①]

隣り合う単語どうしのつながりが強い場合、前の単語の語尾の子音が、後の単語の語頭の母音と結合して発音されることがよくあります。いわゆる「リンキング」と言われる現象です。とくに、前の単語の語尾の子音が [r]、[m]、[n] 音などのときによく起こります。(例：there is, come in, turn on など)

### Example 💿 1-15

You'll see a picture and hear four short statements. Fill in the blanks and choose the statement that best describes what you see in the picture.

(A) All the people are dancing
　　　(　　　)(　　　) gym.

(B) All the people are
　　　(　　　)(　　　) garden.

(C) (　　　) a big dog (　　　)
　　　(　　　) garden.

(D) (　　　) a boy playing the flute.

Ⓐ Ⓑ Ⓒ Ⓓ

## Part 1 Photographs

You'll see a picture and hear four short statements. Choose the statement that best describes what you see in the picture.

**1**

Ⓐ Ⓑ Ⓒ Ⓓ

**2**

Ⓐ Ⓑ Ⓒ Ⓓ

# Part 2  Question - Response  1-18,19,20,21

*You'll hear a question followed by three responses. Choose the best response to each question.*

3. Mark your answer on your answer sheet.  (A)(B)(C)

4. Mark your answer on your answer sheet.  (A)(B)(C)

5. Mark your answer on your answer sheet.  (A)(B)(C)

6. Mark your answer on your answer sheet.  (A)(B)(C)

# Part 3  Conversation  1-22,23

*You'll hear one conversation with three people and read three questions followed by four answers. Choose the best answer to each question.*

7. Why did they decide against going to the French restaurant?
   (A) It's too expensive.
   (B) It's probably too crowded.
   (C) One of the men ate there yesterday.
   (D) The woman ate there a couple of days ago.

   (A)(B)(C)(D)

8. What did the woman say about the Mexican restaurant?
   (A) The restaurant is located on 12th Street.
   (B) She has not eaten there before.
   (C) She always enjoys eating there.
   (D) She ate there yesterday.

   (A)(B)(C)(D)

9. What does the woman mean when she says,"How many times have we been there"?
   (A) She and her colleagues have not eaten at the diner recently.
   (B) She and her colleagues have not eaten at the diner many times.
   (C) She can't remember how many times she has eaten at the diner.
   (D) She would rather not eat at the diner today.

   (A)(B)(C)(D)

# Part 4 Talk 🎧 1-24,25

You'll hear one talk and read three questions about the talk. The questions will be followed by four answers. Choose the best answer to each question.

10. When will dinner be served?
    (A) 4:00
    (B) 5:00
    (C) 6:00
    (D) 7:00

    Ⓐ Ⓑ Ⓒ Ⓓ

11. Look at the picture. Where is the bar?

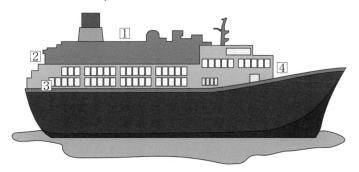

    (A) 1
    (B) 2
    (C) 3
    (D) 4

    Ⓐ Ⓑ Ⓒ Ⓓ

12. What view will people be able to see?
    (A) A view of the moon
    (B) A view of the river
    (C) A view of the mountains
    (D) A view of the sunset

    Ⓐ Ⓑ Ⓒ Ⓓ

---

### TOEIC 攻略のコツ：Part 1
### 音声が流れてくる前に写真から予測しよう

英文が流れる前に写真の内容を確認して英文を予測しておきましょう。主に人物が写っている写真では、人物がどういう動作をしているのか（例：The man is taking a picture.）、どういう状況にいるのか（例：The people are at the table.）を押さえておきましょう。人物のいない写真の場合は、何がどこにあるのか（例：The building stands behind the park.）に焦点をあてましょう。場所を表す前置詞（句）（例：across, along, beside, in front of, next to, through など）を押さえておくとよいでしょう。

# Reading

## 文法問題攻略のポイント：形容詞＆冠詞

1. 形容詞は文中で主格補語や目的格補語になる。
    例1：The chef in that restaurant is **creative** in his use of new ingredients.
        （主語を説明する主格補語）
    例2：The chef in that restaurant considers his job very **challenging**.
        （目的語を説明する目的格補語）
2. 形容詞は（代）名詞の前後に置かれてこれを修飾する。
    例1：**Organic** vegetables are often found in a grocery store.
    例2：Could you give me something **refreshing** to drink?
3. 定冠詞 the は、名詞の前に置かれ、「他にはない唯一のもの」というニュアンスを与える。一般に聞き手にそれとわかるものには、定冠詞を用いる。
    例：Would you pour more wine in **the** glass?
        （不特定のグラスではなく、目の前にある特定のグラスを指している。）

## Part 5 Incomplete Sentences

*A word or phrase is missing in each sentence. Choose the best answer to complete the sentence.*

13. Japanese people's _____ for fish is part of Japanese cultural history.
    (A) prefer
    (B) preference
    (C) preferable
    (D) preferably

    Ⓐ Ⓑ Ⓒ Ⓓ

14. Our restaurant has a lot of _____ patrons, so we do not have to advertise our restaurant in mass media.
    (A) regulation
    (B) regulating
    (C) regulated
    (D) regular

    Ⓐ Ⓑ Ⓒ Ⓓ

15. Eating in a _____ way and doing moderate exercise are good for your health.
    (A) sensitive
    (B) sensible
    (C) sensual
    (D) sense

    Ⓐ Ⓑ Ⓒ Ⓓ

16. Each of the theme restaurants will serve you their _____ specialties.
    (A) respectable
    (B) respectful
    (C) respected
    (D) respective

    Ⓐ Ⓑ Ⓒ Ⓓ

# Part 6 Text Completion

*Read the following text. A word, phrase, or sentence is missing. Choose the best answer to complete the text.*

*Questions 17-19 refer to the following advertisement.*

## Restaurant Guide

Our restaurant is located in the ( 17 ) center of the city, but it is not noisy at all. Bring your important guests to our restaurant for a pleasant time. Our restaurant has eight private rooms for two to ten people as well as counter seating. You can enjoy fresh seafood and ( 18 ) ingredients. We are sure that our food and atmosphere will satisfy your five senses. We offer lunch and dinner from Monday through Saturday. ( 19 ).

17. (A) mere
    (B) very
    (C) only
    (D) sole

18. (A) season
    (B) seasoning
    (C) seasonally
    (D) seasonal

19. (A) We hope you apply to us as soon as possible.
    (B) Thank you for dining in our restaurant.
    (C) If you need some advice, please contact the kitchen staff.
    (D) We recommend that you make a reservation, especially on weekends.

# Part 7 Reading Comprehension (Double Passages)

*Read the following texts. Each text or set of texts is followed by several questions. Choose the best answer to each question.*

*Questions 20-24 refer to the following Web page and review.*

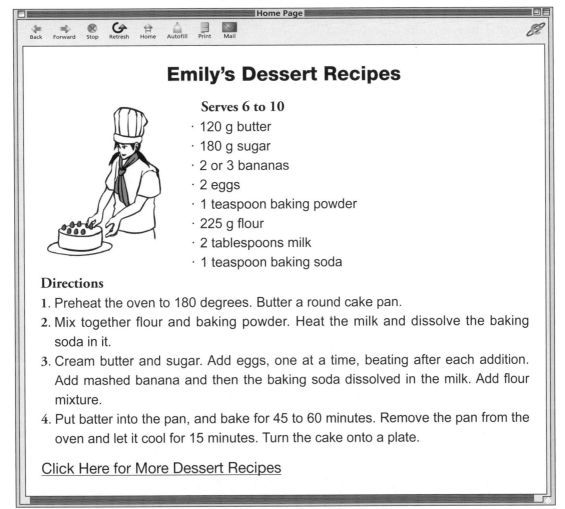

## Emily's Dessert Recipes

**Serves 6 to 10**
- 120 g butter
- 180 g sugar
- 2 or 3 bananas
- 2 eggs
- 1 teaspoon baking powder
- 225 g flour
- 2 tablespoons milk
- 1 teaspoon baking soda

### Directions

1. Preheat the oven to 180 degrees. Butter a round cake pan.
2. Mix together flour and baking powder. Heat the milk and dissolve the baking soda in it.
3. Cream butter and sugar. Add eggs, one at a time, beating after each addition. Add mashed banana and then the baking soda dissolved in the milk. Add flour mixture.
4. Put batter into the pan, and bake for 45 to 60 minutes. Remove the pan from the oven and let it cool for 15 minutes. Turn the cake onto a plate.

Click Here for More Dessert Recipes

### Review by Amy

I've tried several recipes and this is the best banana cake I've ever made. Last week I had a potluck party and was asked to bring dessert. I had some ripe bananas at home, so I decided to make a banana cake. I searched the Internet, and decided to use Emily's Dessert Recipes, which I often refer to. This time I made some arrangements. I cut some of the sugar because I am on a diet. I also replaced the butter with coconut oil to limit calorie intake. I didn't have any baking soda at home, so I didn't use it. I baked it for 60 minutes and finally I had a fabulous banana cake. My friends at the party enjoyed it and asked me for the recipe.

20. What is this recipe for?
 (A) Banana cookies
 (B) Banana pudding
 (C) Banana cake
 (D) Banana shake

21. Which of the following information is NOT included in this recipe?
 (A) How long the cake should be baked.
 (B) How many people the cake can be shared among.
 (C) How the cake should be cooled.
 (D) How the cake tastes.

22. Which of the following is mentioned in this recipe?
 (A) You should combine flour and baking powder.
 (B) You should add all the eggs at the same time.
 (C) You cannot get this recipe on the Internet.
 (D) You can make a variety of cakes with this recipe.

23. Why did Amy decide to make this dessert?
 (A) She had some bananas at home.
 (B) She was asked to make a side dish.
 (C) She likes cakes very much.
 (D) She wanted to refer to Emily's Dessert Recipes.

24. What ingredient did Amy actually use?
 (A) cream
 (B) baking powder
 (C) baking soda
 (D) butter

ⒶⒷⒸⒹ

# **E**xpand your vocabulary! ―接尾辞で品詞がわかる！【形容詞】

➢ **-able / -ible**「～できる」（例：eatable, edible）
➢ **-ic**「～の、～的」（例：economic, domestic）
➢ **-ed**［動詞の過去分詞が形容詞となっている］（例：excited, amazed）
➢ **-ant / -ent**［動詞の現在分詞に対応する形容詞］（例：reliant, insistent）
➢ **-ful**「～に満ちた」（例：harmful, doubtful）
➢ **-ing**［動詞の現在分詞が形容詞となっている］（例：exciting, amazing）
➢ **-ive**「～の、～の性質をもつ」（例：attractive, conservative）
➢ **-less**「～のない」（例：careless, harmless）
➢ **-ous**「～を有する、～の多い」（例：populous, numerous）

# **L**earn more! ― **V**ocabulary in Context

*Complete each English sentence according to its Japanese translation. The first letter is given.*

**1.** Please (r⎵⎵⎵⎵) from (s⎵⎵⎵⎵) in this restaurant.
 （このレストランでは喫煙はご遠慮ください。）

**2.** I would like to express my (g⎵⎵⎵⎵) for your cordial (h⎵⎵⎵⎵).
 （心からのもてなしに感謝の意を表したいと思います。）

**3.** ― What would you like to have as an (a⎵⎵⎵⎵)?
 ― I don't have much of an (a⎵⎵⎵⎵), so I'll just have a salad.
 （―前菜は何がよろしいですか？）
 （―食欲がありませんので、サラダだけいただきます。）

**4.** What accompanying (d⎵⎵⎵⎵) comes with today's (s⎵⎵⎵⎵)?
 （今日の特別料理の付け合せは何ですか？）

---

1. refrain, smoking 2. gratitude, hospitality 3. appetizer, appetite 4. dish, special

# Unit 3
## Medicine & Health

このユニットでは、医療や健康のトピックを扱います。私たちの生活と切り離せないこれらのトピックは TOEIC テストにもよく出題されます。

■ **Vocabulary** *Match each English word with its meaning in Japanese.* 1-26

| | | |
|---|---|---|
| 1. annual ( ) | 2. cancer ( ) | 3. checkup ( ) |
| 4. component ( ) | 5. conduct ( ) | 6. counselor ( ) |
| 7. deadline ( ) | 8. disease ( ) | 9. eventually ( ) |
| 10. explore ( ) | 11. facility ( ) | 12. factor ( ) |
| 13. feature ( ) | 14. impact ( ) | 15. nutrition ( ) |

a. 影響　　b. 栄養　　c. 行なう・指揮する・案内する・行為　　d. 癌　　e. 結局
f. 健康診断　　g. 施設　　h. 締切　　i. 成分　　j. 相談相手　　k. 調査する
l. 特徴・呼び物にする　　m. 病気　　n. 毎年の　　o. 要素

■ **Word Pairs** *Fill in each blank to complete the sentences.*

1. Her father died of a (　　　　　)(　　　　　) last year.

2. I (　　　　　)(　　　　　) hay fever in spring every year.

3. They have started a campaign to (　　　　　)(　　　　　) of the AIDS threat.

4. She has (　　　　　)(　　　　　) the disease. Now she is fine.

5. She does exercise every weekend to (　　　　　) in good (　　　　　).

| | | |
|---|---|---|
| a. keep / shape | b. suffer / from | c. heart / attack |
| d. recovered / from | e. raise / awareness | |

# Listening

## Listening Skill：音の変化に気をつけよう(3) ［子音と母音の連結②］

子音と母音の連結についてさらに練習しましょう。Unit2 で触れた［r］、［m］、［n］音以外の子音も、次にくる単語の母音としばしば連結します。（例：call on, drop in, make up, put on など）

## Example 1-27

*You'll see a picture and hear four short statements. Fill in the blanks and choose the statement that best describes what you see in the picture.*

(A) The people are (　　　)(　　　) line.

(B) The people are (　　　)(　　　) the road.

(C) The people are (　　　　).

(D) The people are (　　　)(　　　).

Ⓐ Ⓑ Ⓒ Ⓓ

## Part 1 Photographs

*You'll see a picture and hear four short statements. Choose the statement that best describes what you see in the picture.*

**1**  1-28

Ⓐ Ⓑ Ⓒ Ⓓ

**2**  1-29

Ⓐ Ⓑ Ⓒ Ⓓ

# Part 2 Question - Response  (CD)1-30,31,32,33

*You'll hear a question followed by three responses. Choose the best response to each question.*

3. Mark your answer on your answer sheet.  Ⓐ Ⓑ Ⓒ

4. Mark your answer on your answer sheet.  Ⓐ Ⓑ Ⓒ

5. Mark your answer on your answer sheet.  Ⓐ Ⓑ Ⓒ

6. Mark your answer on your answer sheet.  Ⓐ Ⓑ Ⓒ


# Part 3 Conversation  (CD)1-34,35

*You'll hear one conversation between two people and read three questions followed by four answers. Choose the best answer to each question.*

7. Why does the man want to start exercising?
   (A) He wants to start weightlifting.
   (B) He wants to learn to swim.
   (C) He wants to lose weight.
   (D) He wants to train for a marathon.

   Ⓐ Ⓑ Ⓒ Ⓓ

8. What did the woman mention as a good point of the sports club?
   (A) The club members are very friendly.
   (B) The price is very reasonable.
   (C) There is a lot of exercise equipment.
   (D) The trainers are very helpful.

   Ⓐ Ⓑ Ⓒ Ⓓ

9. What does the man think might be a problem with the sports club?
   (A) He thinks it does not have good facilities.
   (B) He thinks it might be crowded.
   (C) He thinks it might be expensive.
   (D) He thinks it closes early in the evenings.

   Ⓐ Ⓑ Ⓒ Ⓓ

# Part 4 Talk 🎧1-36,37

*You'll hear one talk and read three questions about the talk. The questions will be followed by four answers. Choose the best answer to each question.*

10. What is being advertised?
   (A) A hospital
   (B) A sports center
   (C) A vacation resort
   (D) A health food store

   Ⓐ Ⓑ Ⓒ Ⓓ

11. What good feature of the Pine Tree Inn is mentioned?
   (A) You can go sightseeing there.
   (B) You can go hiking there.
   (C) You can get a counselor's license there.
   (D) You can learn how to eat more healthily there.

   Ⓐ Ⓑ Ⓒ Ⓓ

12. What will the nutrition counselors do?
   (A) They will measure your current level of fitness.
   (B) They will help you design an eating plan.
   (C) They will help you design an exercise plan.
   (D) They will help you discover how to relax.

   Ⓐ Ⓑ Ⓒ Ⓓ

---

## TOEIC 攻略のコツ：Parts 2
## Yes/No疑問文に Yes/No で答えない表現に注意

Part 2の設問には Wh 疑問文、付加疑問文や Yes/No疑問文が含まれます。Yes/No疑問文では、Yes/No で答えない場合があるので注意しましょう。例えば、Will you go to Amy's party? に対して、I haven't decided yet. と明確に回答しなかったり、Did you get there by taxi? に対して、A friend of mine gave me a lift. と答えたりします。また、Is Tom a good employee? に対して Absolutely. などの口語的な表現を使う場合もあります。紋切り型ではない返答もあることを覚えておきましょう。

# Reading

## 文法問題攻略のポイント：副詞

1. 副詞には、動詞、形容詞、副詞、文全体を修飾する働きがある。
   例1：The doctor <u>looked after</u> the patient **intensively**.
   例2：**Fortunately,** <u>he recovered from cancer</u>.
2. 文における副詞の位置は、比較的自由である。ただし、頻度を表す副詞の場合は、一般に、普通動詞の前、be 動詞や助動詞の後である。
   例1：He **usually** goes jogging in the morning to keep in good shape.
   例2：I have **never** had the flu in my life.
3. -ly の有無で意味が異なる副詞がある。
   hard（激しく、熱心に）/ hardly（ほとんど〜ない）, late（遅く）/ lately（最近） など
4. 特定の動詞や形容詞などとともによく使われる副詞がある。
   look closely, work cooperatively, currently under construction,
   temporarily closed, respond promptly, extremely successful など

## Part 5 Incomplete Sentences

*A word or phrase is missing in each sentence. Choose the best answer to complete the sentence.*

13. She has been suffering from a backache ____.
    (A) late
    (B) lately
    (C) later
    (D) last

14. I am very healthy. I _____ in the hospital.
    (A) have been
    (B) was never being
    (C) have never been
    (D) had never been

15. _____, he succeeded in losing five kilograms in one month.
    (A) Surprise
    (B) Surprised
    (C) Surprising
    (D) Surprisingly

16. I _____ go to the gym and work out after work.
    (A) every day
    (B) on week days
    (C) often
    (D) most

## Part 6 Text Completion

*Read the following text. A word, phrase, or sentence is missing. Choose the best answer to complete the text.*

*Questions 17-19 refer to the following article.*

# World No-Tobacco Day

In 1989, the World Health Organization (WHO) created World No Tobacco Day on May 31st, to raise public awareness about the health impact of smoking. Tobacco is the second major cause of death in the world. (    17    ).
It is said that half the people who smoke (    18    ) today will eventually die from tobacco use. Another (    19    ) alarming fact is that hundreds of thousands of people who have never smoked die every year from diseases caused by breathing second-hand tobacco smoke.

17. (A) Another major cause of death is malnutrition.
    (B) Most people dislike tobacco smoke.
    (C) Tobacco causes serious diseases such as heart attack and cancer.
    (D) One component of tobacco is nicotine.

    Ⓐ Ⓑ Ⓒ Ⓓ

18. (A) regulation
    (B) regularity
    (C) regular
    (D) regularly

    Ⓐ Ⓑ Ⓒ Ⓓ

19. (A) hardly
    (B) cooperatively
    (C) equally
    (D) tightly

    Ⓐ Ⓑ Ⓒ Ⓓ

# Part 7 Reading Comprehension (Single Passages)

*Read the following texts. Each text or set of texts is followed by several questions. Choose the best answer to each question.*

*Questions 20-22 refer to the following article.*

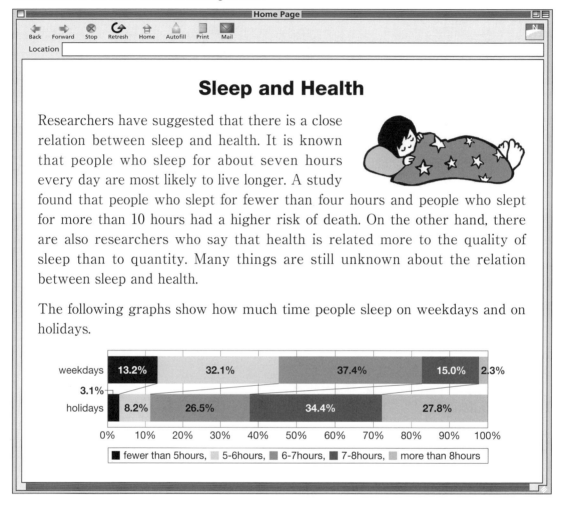

20. What is true about the findings of the research exploring the relation between sleep and health?
(A) The longer you sleep, the longer you will live.
(B) The longer you sleep, the higher risk of death you will have.
(C) People who sleep for seven hours every day are more likely to live longer than those who sleep for four hours.
(D) People who sleep for 10 hours every day are more likely to live longer than those who sleep for seven hours.

Ⓐ Ⓑ Ⓒ Ⓓ

21. What is true about the passage?
   (A) Every researcher believes that the amount of sleep is the most important factor for health.
   (B) Every researcher believes that the amount of sleep is not related to health at all.
   (C) Every researcher believes that there is no relationship between sleep and health.
   (D) Not everything is clear about the relation between sleep and health.

22. What is true about the graphs?
   (A) On weekdays, the percentage of people who sleep for seven to eight hours is the highest.
   (B) On weekdays, the percentage of people who sleep for fewer than six hours is higher than that of people who sleep for more than six hours.
   (C) On holidays, more than 30 percent of people sleep for over eight hours.
   (D) More than 10 percent of people sleep for fewer than six hours even on holidays.

*Questions 23-24 refer to the following memo.*

To: All staff
From: Roger Anderson, Personnel Department
Subject: Annual health checkup

This year, a physical checkup will be conducted at the Youth Center near our office. It will be held between April 16 and April 30, from 9:00 till 12:00. Dates or times cannot be reserved. Please visit the Youth Center when it is convenient for you. If you do not want to wait for a long time, we recommend you avoid coming on the final day when it is expected to be very crowded.—[1]—

The checkup includes height and weight measurement, blood test, urine check, chest X-ray, blood pressure check, eyesight exam and a brief interview by a doctor.—[2]—

Please visit the Personnel Department and sign up for a checkup by next Monday and do not forget to take an application form there.—[3]—

If you have any questions about the checkup, do not hesitate to contact the Personnel Department.—[4]—

Kind regards,

Roger Anderson
Manager
Personnel Department

**23.** What information is NOT included in the memo?

  (A) The dates and times an annual health checkup will be held

  (B) The deadline for registration for a health checkup

  (C) The items included in a health checkup

  (D) The items included in an application form for a health checkup

Ⓐ Ⓑ Ⓒ Ⓓ

**24.** In which of the positions marked[1], [2], [3] and [4] does the following sentence best belong?

  "It will save you time if you fill in the form before you go to the Youth Center."

(A) [1]    (B) [2]    (C) [3]    (D) [4]

Ⓐ Ⓑ Ⓒ Ⓓ

・・・・・・・・・・・・・・・・・・・・・・・・・・・

# Ｅxpand your vocabulary! ─接尾辞で品詞がわかる！【動詞・副詞】

■動詞の代表的な接尾辞は以下のとおり。

➢ **-en**（例：strengthen, broaden）

➢ **-fy**（例：satisfy, classify）

➢ **-ize**（例：organize, memorize）

■副詞の代表的な接尾辞は以下のとおり。

➢ **-ly**（例：generally, easily）

＊ただし、friendly は通常形容詞、lovely、daily、weekly、monthly は形容詞と副詞の両方に使われます。

# Ｌearn more! ─ Ｖocabulary in Context

*Complete each English sentence according to its Japanese translation. The first letter is given.*

**1.** This medical (i      ) covers medical (t      ) for illness and injury.

  （この医療保険は、病気や怪我による治療に適用されます。）

**2.** Some medicines can cause serious (s      )(e      ).

  （重大な副作用を引き起こしうる薬もある。）

**3.** An (a      ) reaction may produce harmful (s      ).

  （アレルギー反応は有害な症状を引き起こすこともある。）

**4.** I'll write out a (p      ) and you can have it (f      ) at a drugstore.

  （処方箋を書きますので、薬局で調剤してもらって下さい。）

1. insurance, treatment  2. side effects  3. allergic, symptoms  4. prescription, filled

# Unit 4
## Traffic & Travel

ビジネスマンはいろいろな交通手段を使って職場に通います。また、出張で出かけることもあれば、日常を離れ休暇を取って旅行することもあります。このユニットでは、交通機関や旅行に関する英語表現を学びましょう。

## ■ Vocabulary  *Match each English word with its meaning in Japanese.* 🎵1-38

| | | |
|---|---|---|
| 1. apologize ( ) | 2. architect ( ) | 3. astronomy ( ) |
| 4. beverage ( ) | 5. boarding pass ( ) | 6. book ( ) |
| 7. brochure ( ) | 8. courier ( ) | 9. delay ( ) |
| 10. fare ( ) | 11. frequent ( ) | 12. intersection ( ) |
| 13. pedestrian ( ) | 14. purse ( ) | 15. souvenir ( ) |

**a.** 謝る  **b.** 運賃  **c.** 建築家  **d.** 交差点  **e.** 宅配業者  **f.** 遅延（させる）

**g.** 天文学  **h.** 搭乗券  **i.** 飲み物  **j.** ハンドバッグ  **k.** パンフレット

**l.** 頻繁な  **m.** 歩行者  **n.** みやげ  **o.** 予約する

## ■ Word Pairs  *Fill in each blank to complete the sentences.*

1. I hope that I will be able to visit all the places (            ) my (            ).

2. He had to (            )(            ) in London after leaving Rome, which meant going to the other terminal, showing his passport, and opening his bag again.

3. Is there a (            )(            ) office around here?

4. How far in advance is it necessary to (            ) a (            ) from Tokyo to London?

5. Flight details include (            )(            ) and aircraft type, as well as the forecasted weather conditions for your selected destination.

| | | |
|---|---|---|
| **a.** departure / time | **b.** on / itinerary | **c.** stop / over |
| **d.** commuter / ticket | **e.** reserve / flight | |

# Listening

## Listening Skill：音の変化に気をつけよう(4)　[音の混合]

前の単語が［d］、［t］、［s］、［z］音などで終わり、次に［j］音の「y」で始まる単語がくる場合に、2つの子音が混合して別の音になる場合があります。（例：di<u>d y</u>ou, mee<u>t y</u>ou, mi<u>ss y</u>ou, a<u>s y</u>ou know など）

### Example 🎵1-39

*You'll hear a question followed by three responses. Fill in the blanks and choose the best response to the question.*

(　　　)(　　　　) please (　　　　)(　　　　　) luggage on this counter?

(A) No, not at all.
(B) Yes. May I see your boarding pass?
(C) Sure. This purse, too?

Ⓐ Ⓑ Ⓒ

## Part 1 Photographs

*You'll see a picture and hear four short statements. Choose the statement that best describes what you see in the picture.*

**1**

Ⓐ Ⓑ Ⓒ Ⓓ

**2**

Ⓐ Ⓑ Ⓒ Ⓓ

# Part 2 Question - Response 🔊 1-42,43,44,45

*You'll hear a question followed by three responses. Choose the best response to each question.*

3. Mark your answer on your answer sheet.          Ⓐ Ⓑ Ⓒ

4. Mark your answer on your answer sheet.          Ⓐ Ⓑ Ⓒ

5. Mark your answer on your answer sheet.          Ⓐ Ⓑ Ⓒ

6. Mark your answer on your answer sheet.          Ⓐ Ⓑ Ⓒ


# Part 3 Conversation 🔊 1-46,47

*You'll hear one conversation between two people and read three questions followed by four answers. Choose the best answer to each question.*

7. What time does the plane leave?
   (A) 7:00 AM
   (B) 7:15 AM
   (C) 7:30 AM
   (D) 7:50 AM                                    Ⓐ Ⓑ Ⓒ Ⓓ

8. What is the man's job?
   (A) Flight attendant
   (B) Traffic officer
   (C) Airline pilot
   (D) Travel agent                               Ⓐ Ⓑ Ⓒ Ⓓ

9. Where is the woman going?
   (A) Tokyo
   (B) Bangkok
   (C) London
   (D) Madrid                                     Ⓐ Ⓑ Ⓒ Ⓓ

# Part 4 Talk 1-48,49

*You'll hear one talk and read three questions about the talk. The questions will be followed by four answers. Choose the best answer to each question.*

10. Where is this talk taking place?
   (A) On a bus
   (B) On a plane
   (C) On a boat
   (D) In a taxi

   Ⓐ Ⓑ Ⓒ Ⓓ

11. What does the speaker mean when he says "we couldn't ask for better weather today, could we"?
   (A) He would like to know people's opinion about the weather.
   (B) He is apologizing for today's bad weather.
   (C) He wishes the weather were better today.
   (D) He thinks the weather is good today.

   Ⓐ Ⓑ Ⓒ Ⓓ

12. What can people buy at the final stop?
   (A) Drinks
   (B) Lunch
   (C) Gifts
   (D) Dinner

   Ⓐ Ⓑ Ⓒ Ⓓ

---

### TOEIC 攻略のコツ：Parts 3-4
### 音声が流れてくる前に Key Words から内容を予測しよう

Parts 3-4では、プリントされている設問や解答の選択肢が大きなヒントになります。音声が流れてくる前に、これらに素早く目を通し、key words（日時・場所・数字など）を確認しておきましょう。そうすることで、内容を推測でき、また正解を探りながら音声を聞くことができます。ただし、設問と選択肢の両方に目を通す時間がない場合は、どちらか片方に決めて目を通しましょう。

# Reading

## 文法問題攻略のポイント：比較

1. 同等比較　as ＋ 形容詞・副詞の原級 ＋ as ～
    例：New York City is **as crowded as** Tokyo.
2. 比較級　形容詞・副詞 ＋ er than ～ または、more ＋ 形容詞・副詞 than ～ など
    例１：Planes are **faster than** super-express trains.
    例２：London is **more expensive than** Tokyo.
3. 最上級　the 形容詞・副詞 ＋ est または、the most ＋ 形容詞・副詞 ＋（of ＋ 複数名詞・in ＋ 場所など）
    例１：Wyoming has **the smallest** population **of** all the **states**.
    例２：Football is **the most popular** sport **in the United States**.
4. 比較級の強調には much や a lot など、最上級の強調には very や by far などが用いられる。
    例：Flying is **much** more comfortable than going by ferry.

## Part 5 Incomplete Sentences

*A word or phrase is missing in each sentence. Choose the best answer to complete the sentence.*

13. This travel brochure says that Italy is one of _____ foreign countries for Japanese tourists to visit.
    (A) the most popular
    (B) popular
    (C) most popularly
    (D) more popular

14. This journey takes you to the Boston Museum, which is _____ than any other museum in this city, with a lot of works of art from many cultures.
    (A) large
    (B) larger
    (C) the larger
    (D) the largest

15. The longer you stay in this hotel, _____ rate you pay for each night.
    (A) low
    (B) the lowest
    (C) lower
    (D) the lower

16. We offer the _____ best accommodations in town.
    (A) much
    (B) more
    (C) very
    (D) far

# Part 6 Text Completion

*Read the following text. A word, phrase, or sentence is missing. Choose the best answer to complete the text.*

*Questions 17-19 refer to the following guide.*

## Tom's Hotel Guide

If you are planning to spend a weekend in San Francisco, here are three good hotels I recommend. Try Atkins Hotel on Main Avenue and you can ask for free upgrades. (   17   ). However, the downtown area can be a little noisy, so if you would like to stay in (   18   ) quieter surroundings, visit All Seasons Hotel. The hotel faces the beach and you can enjoy the best view in town. If you are a frequent traveler to San Francisco, Mountain Hotel is the best. I stayed there (   19   ) ten times and would like to keep going back. The room rate is reasonable, and the service is great. When you stay there, be sure to have a romantic dinner at the hotel's French restaurant.

17. (A) Free upgrades are available on weekdays only.
    (B) If you are lucky, you can find a more gorgeous hotel.
    (C) If you are lucky, you can stay in a suite with a jacuzzi.
    (D) You are likely to stay there free of charge.

    Ⓐ Ⓑ Ⓒ Ⓓ

18. (A) more
    (B) very
    (C) so
    (D) a lot

    Ⓐ Ⓑ Ⓒ Ⓓ

19. (A) at most
    (B) at best
    (C) at last
    (D) at least

    Ⓐ Ⓑ Ⓒ Ⓓ

# Part 7 Reading Comprehension (Single Passages)

*Read the following texts. Each text or set of texts is followed by several questions. Choose the best answer to each question.*

Questions 20-22 refer to the following advertisement and an application form.

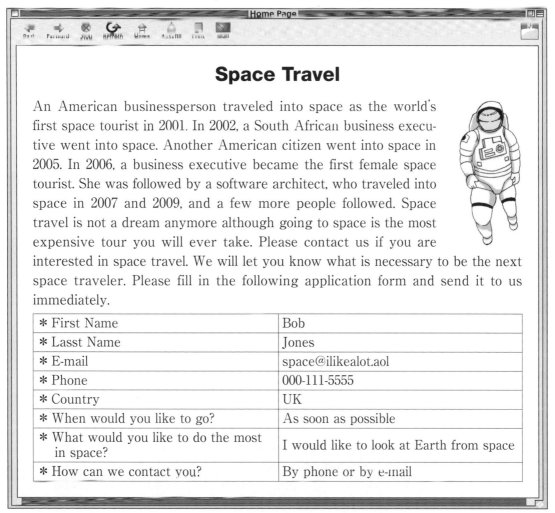

## Space Travel

An American businessperson traveled into space as the world's first space tourist in 2001. In 2002, a South African business executive went into space. Another American citizen went into space in 2005. In 2006, a business executive became the first female space tourist. She was followed by a software architect, who traveled into space in 2007 and 2009, and a few more people followed. Space travel is not a dream anymore although going to space is the most expensive tour you will ever take. Please contact us if you are interested in space travel. We will let you know what is necessary to be the next space traveler. Please fill in the following application form and send it to us immediately.

| * First Name | Bob |
| * Lasst Name | Jones |
| * E-mail | space@ilikealot.aol |
| * Phone | 000-111-5555 |
| * Country | UK |
| * When would you like to go? | As soon as possible |
| * What would you like to do the most in space? | I would like to look at Earth from space |
| * How can we contact you? | By phone or by e-mail |

20. According to the passage, how many people have been to space as tourists so far?
 (A) Fewer than three
 (B) As many as four
 (C) Fewer than Five
 (D) More than five

21. What kind of job did the second space tourist have?
 (A) Architect
 (B) Computer programmer
 (C) Businessperson
 (D) Travel agent                            Ⓐ Ⓑ Ⓒ Ⓓ

22. What information can you get if you send in this application form?
 (A) Information about space tourism
 (B) Information about the people who went into space
 (C) Information about the space industry
 (D) Information about astronomy              Ⓐ Ⓑ Ⓒ Ⓓ

*Questions 23-24 refer to the following online chat discussion.*

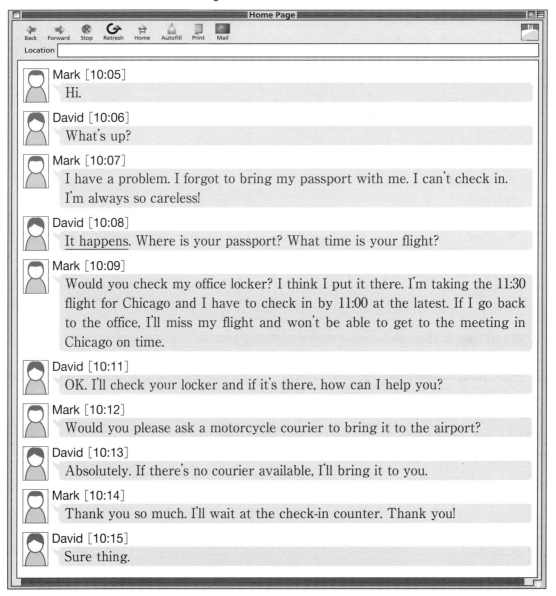

Mark [10:05]
Hi.

David [10:06]
What's up?

Mark [10:07]
I have a problem. I forgot to bring my passport with me. I can't check in. I'm always so careless!

David [10:08]
It happens. Where is your passport? What time is your flight?

Mark [10:09]
Would you check my office locker? I think I put it there. I'm taking the 11:30 flight for Chicago and I have to check in by 11:00 at the latest. If I go back to the office, I'll miss my flight and won't be able to get to the meeting in Chicago on time.

David [10:11]
OK. I'll check your locker and if it's there, how can I help you?

Mark [10:12]
Would you please ask a motorcycle courier to bring it to the airport?

David [10:13]
Absolutely. If there's no courier available, I'll bring it to you.

Mark [10:14]
Thank you so much. I'll wait at the check-in counter. Thank you!

David [10:15]
Sure thing.

23. What is David likely to do first?

 (A) Text to Mark

 (B) Check Mark's locker

 (C) Find a courier

 (D) Go to the airport              Ⓐ Ⓑ Ⓒ Ⓓ

24. At 10：08, what does David mean when he writes, "It happens"?

 (A) David thinks Mark is careless as always.

 (B) David would like to cheer up Mark.

 (C) David thinks he himself is as careless as David.

 (D) David agrees with Mark's comment.       Ⓐ Ⓑ Ⓒ Ⓓ

• • • • • • • • • • • • • • • • • • • • • • • • •

# ✏ Expand your vocabulary! —接頭辞で単語の意味がわかる！(1)

- ➤ **un-**「反対の」（例：unkind）
- ➤ **non-**「非、無」（例：nonsense）
- ➤ **in- / im-**「反対の」（例：informal）
- ➤ **sur-**「過度に」（例：surpass）
- ➤ **ex-**「外へ」（例：export）
- ➤ **de-**「下へ」（例：descend）
- ➤ **inter-**「間の」（例：international）

- ➤ **ir- / il-**「反対の」（例：irregular, illegal）
- ➤ **dis-**「反対の」（例：dishonest）
- ➤ **super-**「超〜」（例：supernatural）
- ➤ **ultra-**「超〜」（例：ultraviolet）
- ➤ **sub-**「下へ」（例：submarine）
- ➤ **under-**「下に」（例：undergraduate）
- ➤ **trans-**「超えて」（例：transport）

# 📖 Learn more! — Vocabulary in Context

*Complete each English sentence according to its Japanese translation. The first letter is given.*

1. It is difficult to find (l          )(a          ) in New York at this time of the year.

 （この時期のニューヨークで豪華な宿泊施設を見つけることはむずかしい。）

2. As the airport is (c          ) with a lot of tourists in August, we will (p          ) our trip until September.

 （8月中は多くの観光客で空港が混雑しますから、9月まで旅行を延期します。）

3. Choose a (w          ) seat if you want to enjoy the view. Choose an (a          ) seat if you are likely to use the bathroom often.

 （景色をお楽しみになりたい方は窓側の席をお選びください。化粧室を頻繁にお使いになる方は、通路側の席をお選びください。）

4. (R          ) days are based on 24-hour units, starting at the time of pick-up. No (r          ) are payable on cars returned early.

 （レンタル日数は24 時間単位で、貸出時から計算します。予定より早く車を返却されても払い戻しはありません。）

1. luxury, accommodations  2. crowded, postpone  3. window, aisle  4. Rental, refunds

41

# Unit 5
# Ordering & Shipping

商品を注文する方法は様々です。最近では、オンラインサービスが従来の書式や電話での注文にとって替わりつつあります。注文すると商品は宅配業者によって発送され、顧客の手元に届けられます。このユニットでは、注文や輸送に関する様々な英語表現を学びましょう。

## ■ Vocabulary  *Match each English word with its meaning in Japanese.* 1-50

| | | |
|---|---|---|
| 1. commission (　) | 2. customs　(　) | 3. destination　(　) |
| 4. enable　　(　) | 5. excluding (　) | 6. expire　　(　) |
| 7. freight　　(　) | 8. inquire　(　) | 9. obtain　　(　) |
| 10. patience　(　) | 11. promptly (　) | 12. restriction　(　) |
| 13. status　　(　) | 14. via　　(　) | 15. warranty　(　) |

**a.** 可能にさせる　　**b.** 貨物（運送）　　**c.** 期限が切れる　　**d.** 状況　　**e.** すぐに

**f.** 税関　　**g.** 制限　　**h.** 尋ねる　　**i.** 手数料　　**j.** 手に入れる

**k.** ～によって・経由で　　**l.** 忍耐　　**m.** ～を除いて　　**n.** 保証　　**o.** 目的地

## ■ Word Pairs  *Fill in each blank to complete the sentences.*

1. The customer is required to pay the (　　　　)(　　　　) when goods are returned.

2. (　　　　)(　　　　) are used to identify your shipments.

3. After I add all the prices, I can give you a (　　　　)(　　　　).

4. We (　　　　) a lot of (　　　　) every day.

5. He used to (　　　　) a regular (　　　　) with our company.

| | | |
|---|---|---|
| **a.** shipping / charges | **b.** make / deliveries | **c.** place / order |
| **d.** tracking / numbers | **e.** grand / total | |

42

# Listening

## Listening Skill：音の変化に気をつけよう(5)　[ t 音の変化]

[t] は変化しやすい音で、語中や文中で本来とは別の音になることがあります。たとえば、「twenty」が「トゥエニ」と聞こえたり、「butter」が「バラ」と聞こえたりします。また、「got to」は「ガタ」や「ガラ」と聞こえることがあります。

## Example 🎧 1-51

*You'll hear a question followed by three responses. Fill in the blanks and choose the best response to the question.*

Which type of watch would you like to order?

(A) Yes, I (　　　　) it yesterday.
(B) I want a (　　　　) one.
(C) He has (　　　　)(　　　　) buy one.

　　　　　　　　　　　　　　　　　　Ⓐ Ⓑ Ⓒ

## Part 1　Photographs

*You'll see a picture and hear four short statements. Choose the statement that best describes what you see in the picture.*

**1**

Ⓐ Ⓑ Ⓒ Ⓓ

**2**

Ⓐ Ⓑ Ⓒ Ⓓ

# Part 2 Question - Response (⊙)1-54,55,56,57

*You'll hear a question followed by three responses. Choose the best response to each question.*

3. Mark your answer on your answer sheet.          Ⓐ Ⓑ Ⓒ

4. Mark your answer on your answer sheet.          Ⓐ Ⓑ Ⓒ

5. Mark your answer on your answer sheet.          Ⓐ Ⓑ Ⓒ

6. Mark your answer on your answer sheet.          Ⓐ Ⓑ Ⓒ

# Part 3 Conversation (⊙)1-58,59

*You'll hear one conversation between two people and read three questions followed by four answers. Choose the best answer to each question.*

7. What problem does the man mention?
  (A) He did not receive his order.
  (B) He received the wrong color pants.
  (C) He received the wrong size pants.
  (D) He did not receive the correct discount on his order.

                                                    Ⓐ Ⓑ Ⓒ Ⓓ

8. What did the woman ask the man to do?
  (A) To give her his name and address
  (B) To return the pants he received
  (C) To change his original order
  (D) To call again later in the week

                                                    Ⓐ Ⓑ Ⓒ Ⓓ

9. Look at the graphic. What most likely is the man's waist size?

| Men's Pants Sizing Information (centimeters) | | |
|---|---|---|
| Size | Waist | Length |
| X-Small | 72-75 | 76-78 |
| Small | 76-80 | 79-81 |
| Medium | 81-84 | 82-84 |
| Large | 84-87 | 85-88 |
| X-Large | 88-91 | 89-92 |
| XX-Large | 92-96 | 89-92 |

  (A) 83 centimeters
  (B) 85 centimeters
  (C) 89 centimeters
  (D) 93 centimeters

                                                    Ⓐ Ⓑ Ⓒ Ⓓ

# Part 4 Talk 🔊 1-60,61

*You'll hear one talk and read three questions about the talk. The questions will be followed by four answers. Choose the best answer to each question.*

10. What kind of customers does Central Freight Agency serve?
 (A) Business customers only
 (B) Private individuals only
 (C) Business customers and private individuals
 (D) Trucking companies

Ⓐ Ⓑ Ⓒ Ⓓ

11. How many freight companies does Central Freight Agency work with?
 (A) More than 40
 (B) More than 50
 (C) More than 60
 (D) More than 70

Ⓐ Ⓑ Ⓒ Ⓓ

12. What is one good feature of the trucking companies that was mentioned in the advertisement?
 (A) They have insurance.
 (B) They have excellent drivers.
 (C) They are always on time.
 (D) They deliver freight very quickly.

Ⓐ Ⓑ Ⓒ Ⓓ

---

## TOEIC 攻略のコツ：Parts 3-4
## 設問が全体の内容についてなのか部分的内容についてなのか区別しよう

全体を聞かないと解けない設問と、一部のみを聞けば解ける設問があります。前者は、What are the speakers discussing? What is the talk about? What are they probably doing? Why [For what purpose] are they meeting now? など主題・人間関係・理由・目的などを問う設問です。こうした設問は最初に置かれることが多いのですが、全体の状況がわからないと解けないため、後回しにしましょう。部分的内容に関する設問については、会話やトークを聞く前に設問を読んでおけば、その部分の英文が流れたときにピンポイントで正解を選べるはずです。

# Reading

## 文法問題攻略のポイント：動詞＆時制

1. 目的語をとる動詞が他動詞で、とらない動詞が自動詞である。
   例1：We should **discuss** this issue. = We should **talk about** this issue.
   例2：He **opposed** our plan. = He **objected to** our plan.
2. 現在時制は、現在の状態や習慣などを表し頻度を表す副詞（句）とともに用いられることが多い。現在進行中の動作や繰り返し行なわれる動作を表す現在進行形との違いに注意！
   例：Our manager usually **eats** lunch at the cafeteria, but now he **is eating** lunch at the office.
3. 進行形にできない動詞がある。
   例：I **know** [× am knowing] the president of this company.
4. 過去時制と現在完了の違いに注意。
   どちらか一方とのみ用いられる、時を表す語句がある。
   例1："When did he quit his job?" "He quit his job last year."
   例2：He has been working at this company since he quit his previous job.

## Part 5 Incomplete Sentences

*A word or phrase is missing in each sentence. Choose the best answer to complete the sentence.*

13. Currently we ＿＿＿ outside the United States.
    (A) did not ship
    (B) are not shipped
    (C) do not ship
    (D) have not shipped
    Ⓐ Ⓑ Ⓒ Ⓓ

14. A courier ＿＿＿ just now.
    (A) has sent
    (B) is being sent
    (C) is sent
    (D) was sent
    Ⓐ Ⓑ Ⓒ Ⓓ

15. That moving company ＿＿＿ for 20 years and went out of business.
    (A) has lasted
    (B) is lasting
    (C) lasts
    (D) lasted
    Ⓐ Ⓑ Ⓒ Ⓓ

16. All warranty claims must be processed where customers ＿＿＿ the product.
    (A) purchased
    (B) has purchased
    (C) are purchasing
    (D) purchases
    Ⓐ Ⓑ Ⓒ Ⓓ

# Part 6 Text Completion

*Read the following text. A word, phrase, or sentence is missing. Choose the best answer to complete the text.*

*Questions 17-19 refer to the following article.*

## Business Communication

In order to describe sales orders which ( **17** ) yet, avoid using negative sentences in your business letter. For instance, it would be better to state "It will be shipped soon." instead of saying "We have not shipped it yet." It would be ( **18** ) better if you give a reasonable time frame like: ( **19** ) In addition, it is acceptable to use the term "shipment" to refer to any product sent by trains, cars and airplanes.

17. (A) has not been shipped
    (B) have not been shipped
    (C) has not shipped
    (D) have not shipped

Ⓐ Ⓑ Ⓒ Ⓓ

18. (A) very
    (B) so
    (C) more
    (D) much

Ⓐ Ⓑ Ⓒ Ⓓ

19. (A) "The rest of your order will not be shipped very soon."
    (B) "The rest of your order will be shipped within a week."
    (C) "The rest of your order will be staying with us for a certain amount of time."
    (D) "The rest of your order will not be shipped for some time."

Ⓐ Ⓑ Ⓒ Ⓓ

# Part 7 Reading Comprehension (Triple Passages)

*Read the following texts. Each text or set of texts is followed by several questions. Choose the best answer to each question.*

Questions 20-24 refer to the following web information and two e-mails.

## Order Shipment Information

Orders received from Monday through Thursday are shipped on the same day, excluding holidays. Orders received on Fridays, and orders received on Saturdays, Sundays, or holidays will be shipped on the following day. Orders will reach you one day after they are shipped. All customers will receive a package tracking number via email from us. Please use this tracking number to look up information about your order. Customer service representatives are available from Monday through Friday, 9:00 am to 5:00 pm. All shipment-related inquiries made after hours, on weekends, and on holidays will be answered on the following day during business hours. Please fill out the following order form and email us immediately.

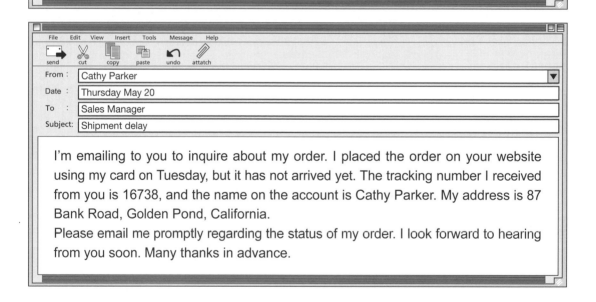

From: Cathy Parker
Date: Thursday May 20
To: Sales Manager
Subject: Shipment delay

I'm emailing to you to inquire about my order. I placed the order on your website using my card on Tuesday, but it has not arrived yet. The tracking number I received from you is 16738, and the name on the account is Cathy Parker. My address is 87 Bank Road, Golden Pond, California.

Please email me promptly regarding the status of my order. I look forward to hearing from you soon. Many thanks in advance.

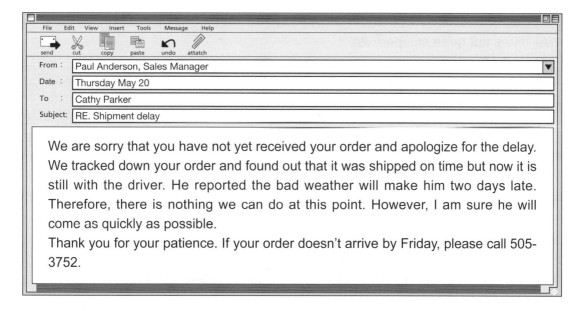

20. Which of the following is true?
   (A) If you send your order on Monday, your order is always shipped on Tuesday.
   (B) If you make an inquiry about your order on Saturday, a customer service representative will help you on the same day.
   (C) If you send your order, a package tracking number will be sent by mail.
   (D) If you have a package tracking number, you will be able to obtain some information about your order.

21. In the first e-mail, the word "status" in line 5 is closest in meaning to
   (A) possibility   (B) probability   (C) situation   (D) classification

22. How did Cathy Parker pay for her order?
   (A) In cash
   (B) By check
   (C) With money orders
   (D) By credit card

23. On what day of the week was Cathy Parker's order shipped?
   (A) Monday   (B) Tuesday   (C) Wednesday   (D) Thursday

**24.** What is most likely true about order #16738?

(A) It has not been shipped yet.

(B) It is with the driver.

(C) It was shipped on Wednesday.

(D) It is not paid for yet.

Ⓐ Ⓑ Ⓒ Ⓓ

## Expand your vocabulary! ──接頭辞で単語の意味がわかる！⑵

➢ **uni-**「１つの」（例：unify, uniform）

➢ **bi-**「２つの」（例：bilingual, bilateral）

➢ **co- / com- / con-**「ともに」
  （例：cooperation, comply, consent）

➢ **counter-**「逆」
  （例：counterpart, counterattack）

➢ **auto-**「自動の」（例：automatic, automobile）

➢ **vice-**「副」
  （例：vice-president, vice-chairperson）

➢ **mis-**「間違った」
  （例：mistake, misunderstanding）

➢ **pre-**「以前の」（例：predict, prewar）

➢ **mono-**「１つの」
  （例：monopoly, monotonous）

➢ **multi-**「多くの」
  （例：multiply, multinational）

➢ **pro-**「前に」（例：progress, proceed）

➢ **post-**「後の」（例：postpone, postwar）

## Learn more! ─ Vocabulary in Context

*Complete each English sentence according to its Japanese translation. The first letter is given.*

1. A merchant (v          ) transports (c          ) and passengers.
   （商船は荷物と乗客を運ぶ。）

2. (C          ) on (d          ) is a financial transaction. You have to pay for products at the time of actual delivery.
   （代金引き換え払いとは、製品が実際に届いたときに支払う金融取引である。）

3. Shipping and handling (c          ) are based on the weight of the (i          ) you order.
   （発送手数料は注文した品目の重量で決まる。）

4. Manufacturers and (d          ) use five basic means of (t          ): air, truck, train, ship, or pipeline.
   （製造業者と流通業者が主に使用する輸送手段は、航空機、トラック、鉄道、船舶、パイプラインの５つである。）

---

1. vessel, cargo　2. Cash, delivery　3. charges, items　4. distributors, transportation

# Unit 6
## Factories & Production

製造業では毎日、色々な製品が工場で数々の工程を経て生産・出荷されています。工場内では、製品はどのように製造され管理されているのでしょうか？このユニットでは、工場や製造に関する様々な英語表現を学びましょう。

## ■ Vocabulary  *Match each English word with its meaning in Japanese.*  🎧1-62

| | | |
|---|---|---|
| 1. appliance ( ) | 2. appreciate ( ) | 3. assembly ( ) |
| 4. bet ( ) | 5. commitment ( ) | 6. contract ( ) |
| 7. defect ( ) | 8. durable ( ) | 9. efficient ( ) |
| 10. fuel ( ) | 11. humidity ( ) | 12. mobility ( ) |
| 13. navigate ( ) | 14. obstacle ( ) | 15. vacuum ( ) |

**a.** 委任・参加　　**b.** 賭ける・賭け　　**c.** 可動性・機動性　　**d.** 感謝する・よさがわかる
**e.** （電気）器具・装置　　**f.** 組み立て・集会　　**g.** 契約・契約を結ぶ　　**h.** 欠点・欠陥
**i.** 効率のいい・能率的な　　**j.** 湿度　　**k.** 障害（物）　　**l.** 操縦する・航行する
**m.** 耐久性のある・丈夫な　　**n.** 電気掃除機で掃除する・真空　　**o.** 燃料

## ■ Word Pairs  *Fill in each blank to complete the sentences.*

1. The materials are sent to the (　　　　　)(　　　　　　　) by a conveyer belt.

2. This electric vehicle does not consume any (　　　　　)(　　　　　).

3. The purpose of (　　　　　)(　　　　　) is to monitor whether products meet specifications.

4. Our newly developed trains are very rapid and (　　　　　)(　　　　　).

5. We import (　　　　　)(　　　　　) mainly from China.

| | | |
|---|---|---|
| **a.** assembly / line | **b.** environmentally / friendly | **c.** fossil / fuel |
| **d.** quality / control | **e.** raw / materials | |

# Listening

## Listening Skill：いろいろな数字に慣れよう！

英語を使って仕事をしていく上で、時間・金額・電話番号・気温などの数字は重要な要素となっています。アメリカやオーストラリアなどでは長さの尺度としてヤード・インチ法が使われているので注意が必要です（1 yard ≒ 0.9144 meter /1 inch ≒ 2.54 centimeters）。また一般にこれらの国では温度に摂氏…度 …℃ (degree(s) Celsius/Centigrade) ではなくて華氏…度 …°F (degree(s) Fahrenheit) が用いられます。(32°F = 0℃)

## Example 1-63

*You'll hear a question followed by three responses. Fill in the blanks and choose the best response to the question.*

What's the temperature in this factory?

(A) It's comfortably controlled at (　　　　)(　　　　).
(B) We maintain (　　　　)(　　　　) humidity in the summertime.
(C) It's May (　　　　).

Ⓐ Ⓑ Ⓒ

# Part 1 Photographs

*You'll see a picture and hear four short statements. Choose the statement that best describes what you see in the picture.*

**1**

Ⓐ Ⓑ Ⓒ Ⓓ

**2**

Ⓐ Ⓑ Ⓒ Ⓓ

# Part 2 Question - Response 🔊 1-66,67,68,69

*You'll hear a question followed by three responses. Choose the best response to each question.*

3. Mark your answer on your answer sheet.     Ⓐ Ⓑ Ⓒ

4. Mark your answer on your answer sheet.     Ⓐ Ⓑ Ⓒ

5. Mark your answer on your answer sheet.     Ⓐ Ⓑ Ⓒ

6. Mark your answer on your answer sheet.     Ⓐ Ⓑ Ⓒ

# Part 3 Conversation 🔊 1-70,71

*You'll hear one conversation with three people and read three questions followed by four answers. Choose the best answer to each question.*

7. Why can't the company reach its production targets?
   (A) The finished products have defects.
   (B) Many employees have been absent this month.
   (C) There is a shortage of raw materials.
   (D) It is difficult to find enough reliable workers.

   Ⓐ Ⓑ Ⓒ Ⓓ

8. What is the woman's suggestion for solving the problem?
   (A) The company should hire extra workers.
   (B) The company should improve its quality control system.
   (C) The company should lower prices for its products.
   (D) The company should purchase raw materials from local sources.

   Ⓐ Ⓑ Ⓒ Ⓓ

9. What is John's opinion about the woman's suggestion for solving the problem?
   (A) The woman's idea would be too expensive.
   (B) Domestic suppliers would not accept the woman's idea.
   (C) The woman's idea is a good solution to the problem.
   (D) The quality control supervisor would not accept the woman's idea.

   Ⓐ Ⓑ Ⓒ Ⓓ

# Part 4 Talk  🎧1-72,73

*You'll hear one talk and read three questions about the talk. The questions will be followed by four answers. Choose the best answer to each question.*

10. What is the first thing that guests on this tour will do?
    (A) Listen to a lecture about the history of Mountaintop Ice Cream
    (B) Take a ten-minute tour of the production facilities
    (C) Take ten minutes to fill out a questionnaire
    (D) Watch a short movie

    Ⓐ Ⓑ Ⓒ Ⓓ

11. What will the tour guides explain?
    (A) How ice cream is made
    (B) The history of Mountaintop Ice Cream
    (C) Mountaintop Ice Cream's commitment to quality
    (D) Mountaintop Ice Cream's special new products

    Ⓐ Ⓑ Ⓒ Ⓓ

12. What does the speaker imply when she says, "Our tour ends just outside the gift shop"?
    (A) Guests should meet near the gift shop after the tour finishes.
    (B) The speaker hopes guests will buy something in the gift shop.
    (C) Guests can return by buses that leave from the gift shop.
    (D) The speaker will offer the guests a free gift after the tour.

    Ⓐ Ⓑ Ⓒ Ⓓ

---

## TOEIC 攻略のコツ：Parts 3-4　Key Words の言い換え表現に着目！

Parts 3-4では、会話の中で使われた表現を同義語などで言い換えて、正解の選択肢としている場合が多くあります。例えば always と all the time, thirty minutes と half an hour、three months と a quarter「四半期」、ten years と a decade などの言い換えがしばしば行なわれます。名詞関連では、colleague と coworker、agreement と contract など、動詞関連では、hand out と distribute、get in touch with と contact などがあります。他に否定語＋反意語で recently と not long ago、disagree と don't think so などもあります。

54

# Reading

## 文法問題攻略のポイント：未来表現など

1. 未来を表すには、be going to ＋ 動詞の原形や will ＋ 動詞の原形などを使う。微妙にニュアンスが違う場合もあるので注意しましょう。
    - 例1：The number of products **will decrease** in a month because our budget is limited.
    - 例2：Our new vacuum cleaners **are going to be** in the market on August 1.
2. 現在形や現在進行形で未来を表すこともある。
    - 例1：Tomorrow **is** our company's foundation day.
    - 例2：We **are having** the test result in a week.
3. 未来時を表す時や条件の副詞節の中では、現在形を使う。
    - 例1：When we **introduce** the nursing-care robots, we won't suffer from a lot of pain and stress.
    - 例2：If you **look** into the insect, you'll be able to get a hint to design a new robot.

## Part 5 Incomplete Sentences

*A word or phrase is missing in each sentence. Choose the best answer to complete the sentence.*

13. A lot of simple labor _____ performed by electric appliances and robots in the course of time.
    - (A) will be
    - (B) is
    - (C) are
    - (D) have been
    Ⓐ Ⓑ Ⓒ Ⓓ

14. Because the government decided to build a new railway station in our city, factories _____ widely, and residential and commercial areas developed around it.
    - (A) have spread
    - (B) spread
    - (C) are spreading
    - (D) will spread
    Ⓐ Ⓑ Ⓒ Ⓓ

15. No casseroles will be made by the company until the order _____ received from consumers.
    - (A) will be
    - (B) is
    - (C) was
    - (D) is going to
    Ⓐ Ⓑ Ⓒ Ⓓ

16. Domestic exports _____ 15 percent last month because of slower sales overseas.
    - (A) fall
    - (B) will fall
    - (C) fell
    - (D) have fallen
    Ⓐ Ⓑ Ⓒ Ⓓ

# Part 6 Text Completion

*Read the following text. A word, phrase, or sentence is missing. Choose the best answer to complete the text.*

*Questions 17-19 refer to the following Web advertisement.*

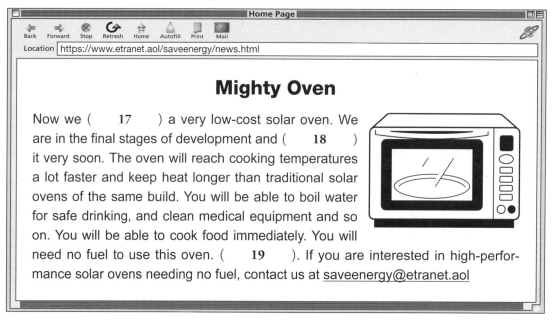

17. (A) develop
    (B) developed
    (C) had developed
    (D) are developing

    Ⓐ Ⓑ Ⓒ Ⓓ

18. (A) launch
    (B) launched
    (C) will be launching
    (D) have launched

    Ⓐ Ⓑ Ⓒ Ⓓ

19. (A) This will truly save a lot of energy.
    (B) This may damage the environment.
    (C) This will contribute to communicating between distant places.
    (D) This will enable a solar car to run longer.

    Ⓐ Ⓑ Ⓒ Ⓓ

# Part 7 Reading Comprehension (Triple Passages)

*Read the following texts. Each text or set of texts is followed by several questions. Choose the best answer to each question.*

*Questions 20-24 refer to the following web advertisement, inquiry and response.*

## iClean

iClean is your best bet if you are ready to get a robot vacuum. How do we know? We made a vacuum track in our factory that allowed us to test robot vacuum cleaners on carpeting, vinyl and wood flooring, spreading dust in their path to see how they would perform. We then took them into a real home to see which ones could navigate around chair legs, under sofas and over flooring changes. We also considered how easy they were to set up and use.

Hundreds of hours of testing later, we had a winner. iClean combines excellent power with ease of movement– an efficient cleaning partner for your home.

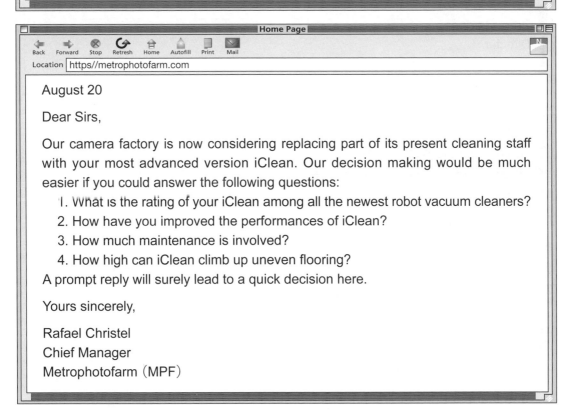

August 20

Dear Sirs,

Our camera factory is now considering replacing part of its present cleaning staff with your most advanced version iClean. Our decision making would be much easier if you could answer the following questions:

1. What is the rating of your iClean among all the newest robot vacuum cleaners?
2. How have you improved the performances of iClean?
3. How much maintenance is involved?
4. How high can iClean climb up uneven flooring?

A prompt reply will surely lead to a quick decision here.

Yours sincerely,

Rafael Christel
Chief Manager
Metrophotofarm (MPF)

August 21

Dear Mr. Rafael Christel,

This is to acknowledge your inquiry of August 20.

Our newest version iClean 7385 is the robot vacuum with the best combination of features overall. It strikes a healthy balance between power and movement for vacuuming around obstacles like chair legs and different levels of flooring. Compared to some other new robot vacuum cleaners, the two newest versions of iClean have features as follows:

| Product | Overall Rating | Performance | Convenience | Design | Support | Climbing Height (Inches) |
|---|---|---|---|---|---|---|
| iClean 7385 | 9.9 | 10 | 10 | 9.9 | 9 | 1.2 |
| Cybervac L230 | 9.7 | 9.8 | 9.5 | 9.8 | 10 | 1.3 |
| Saamba 7101 | 9.6 | 9.5 | 9.5 | 10 | 9 | 1.1 |
| iClean 6204 | 9.3 | 9.3 | 10 | 9.9 | 9 | 1.2 |

We will keep you informed of any changes in our products.

Thank you for your interest in iClean.

Yours sincerely,

Perry Gardner

Director

Fancyelectro Co. Ltd.

20. According to the advertisement, what can iClean do?
 (A) It can be controlled by a smart phone.
 (B) It can react to human voice.
 (C) It can work on different floor types.
 (D) It can clean itself.

21. Which feature of iClean was NOT tested?
 (A) Its usage  (C) Its mobility
 (B) Its vacuum power  (D) Its cleaning-up speed

22. What does Rafael Christel want to know?
 (A) How much the newest iClean costs
 (B) How far the newest iClean can go after a battery charge
 (C) How highly the newest iClean is evaluated
 (D) How long iClean is guaranteed

23. Among the four cleaners, for which feature does Saamba rank highest?
 (A) Appearance  (C) After-sales service
 (B) Ease of use  (D) Efficiency

**24.** Why does Perry Gardner probably mention two different models of iClean?

(A) To show how convenient the newest model has become

(B) To show how high the newest model can go up

(C) To show how much the design of the newest model has been improved

(D) To show how the newest model can work better than the older one

Ⓐ Ⓑ Ⓒ Ⓓ

# Expand your vocabulary! ―多義語に注意しよう！

➤ **account** 名勘定・口座・考慮・説明 動（account for...）…を説明する

➤ **bill** 名請求書・紙幣・法案・ビラ・くちばし 動請求書を送る

➤ **case** 名箱・場合・訴訟・主張

➤ **figure** 名数字・姿・人物 動考える・（figure out）理解する・解く

➤ **interest** 名関心・利子・利害 動興味を持たせる

➤ **mean** 動意味する・つもりである 名平均・（複数形で）方法 形卑劣な

➤ **order** 名命令・注文（品）・秩序 動注文する・命じる

➤ **party** 名パーティー・一行・政党

➤ **plant** 名植物・工場 動植える

➤ **term** 名期間・用語・（複数形で）間柄・条件

# Learn more! ― Vocabulary in Context

*Complete each English sentence according to its Japanese translation. The first letter is given.*

1. Most of the Chinese-made (c                ) imported into Japan are (p                )
(t                ) in our factory.

（日本が輸入している中国製部品の大半が、当工場で組み立てられています。）

2. Many producers of (d                )(g                ) announced production cutbacks last week.

（多くの耐久消費財メーカーが、先週生産削減を発表した。）

3. A (g                )(c                ) has a (s                ) perform a specific task as part of the overall project.

（一般請負業者は下請け業者に総合プロジェクトの一部として特殊な作業を行ってもらっている。）

4. Some (h                )(a                ) manufacturers are increasing their (o                )
of air conditioners because of the expected hot summer.

（暑い夏が予想されるために、エアコンを増産している家庭用電子器具メーカーもある。）

--------

1. components / put / together 2. durable / goods 3. general / contractor / subcontractor
4. household / appliance / output

# Unit 7
# Research & Development

このユニットでは、研究開発、いわゆるＲ＆Ｄについてのトピックを扱います。科学技術の進歩が驚くべき速さで進む現代では、多くの企業や団体が研究開発やマーケティングに力を注いでいます。

## ■ Vocabulary  *Match each English word with its meaning in Japanese.* 🎧 1-74

| | | |
|---|---|---|
| 1. affect ( ) | 2. analyze ( ) | 3. biological ( ) |
| 4. burden ( ) | 5. chemical ( ) | 6. compliant ( ) |
| 7. confidential ( ) | 8. genetic ( ) | 9. hypothesis ( ) |
| 10. investigate ( ) | 11. involve ( ) | 12. laboratory (lab) ( ) |
| 13. procedure ( ) | 14. recommendation ( ) | 15. substance ( ) |

**a.** 遺伝の・遺伝子の・(-s) 遺伝学　　**b.** 影響を及ぼす・作用する
**c.** 化学の・化学物質・薬品　　**d.** 仮説・前提　　**e.** 機密の・信任の厚い
**f.** 実験室・研究室　　**g.** 遵守（じゅんしゅ）する・言いなりになる　　**h.** 推薦・推薦状
**i.** 生物学の　　**j.** 調査する・取り調べる　　**k.** 手続き・手順　　**l.** 伴う・巻き込む
**m.** 荷物・負担・負担させる　　**n.** 物質・実質　　**o.** 分析する

## ■ Word Pairs  *Fill in each blank to complete the sentences.*

1. They decided to ( ) a ( ) to find out public opinion on the issue.

2. The scholar ( ) a new ( ) after observing the house trembling.

3. The recent study ( ) the ( ) that could cause the disease.

4. He did field research to ( ) his opponents' ( ).

5. We ( ) an ( ) to prove that we were correct.

| | | |
|---|---|---|
| **a.** conducted / experiment | **b.** proposed / theory | **c.** explored / factors |
| **d.** take / poll | **e.** challenge / hypothesis | |

# Listening

## Listening Skill：英語とカタカナ表記との発音の違いを認識しよう。

現在の日本語には非常に多くの外来語が入っています。しかし、カタカナで表記されると本来の発音とは異なってしまうため、知っている単語でも音声では聞き取れないことがあります。たとえば animal は日本語ではアニマルと表記されますが、英語音声では「エニモゥ」のように聞こえます。この違いを認識しましょう。

### Example 🔊 1-75

*You'll hear a question followed by three responses. Fill in the blanks and choose the best response to the question.*

**Question**: Where do you keep the (　　　)(　　　)?

(A) I've got a house (　　　)(　　　).
(B) It's next to the (　　　)(　　　).
(C) I spilt it over my (　　　).

Ⓐ Ⓑ Ⓒ

## Part 1 Photographs

*You'll see a picture and hear four short statements. Choose the statement that best describes what you see in the picture.*

**1** 🔊 1-76

Ⓐ Ⓑ Ⓒ Ⓓ

**2** 🔊 1-77

Ⓐ Ⓑ Ⓒ Ⓓ

# Part 2 Question - Response 1-78,79,80,81

*You'll hear a question followed by three responses. Choose the best response to each question.*

3. Mark your answer on your answer sheet.     Ⓐ Ⓑ Ⓒ

4. Mark your answer on your answer sheet.     Ⓐ Ⓑ Ⓒ

5. Mark your answer on your answer sheet.     Ⓐ Ⓑ Ⓒ

6. Mark your answer on your answer sheet.     Ⓐ Ⓑ Ⓒ

# Part 3 Short Conversation 1-82,83

*You'll hear one conversation between two people and read three questions followed by four answers. Choose the best answer to each question.*

7. What are the speakers discussing?
   (A) New products
   (B) Money
   (C) Advertising
   (D) Tax increases

   Ⓐ Ⓑ Ⓒ Ⓓ

8. What does the woman imply when she says, "I'm surprised he's decided to take our advice for a change"?
   (A) She is happy that the director has provided good advice.
   (B) The director should be changed.
   (C) The director does not usually follow the speakers' recommendations.
   (D) She believes that the director should make a different proposal.

   Ⓐ Ⓑ Ⓒ Ⓓ

9. What does the woman want to do?
   (A) Fire an employee
   (B) Increase the advertising budget
   (C) Buy new office equipment
   (D) Employ a new worker

   Ⓐ Ⓑ Ⓒ Ⓓ

62

# Part 4 Talk  1-84,85

*You'll hear one talk and read three questions about the talk. The questions will be followed by four answers. Choose the best answer to each question.*

**10.** Who is the audience for this talk?
  (A) Tourists   (B) Journalists   (C) Doctors   (D) Accountants

Ⓐ Ⓑ Ⓒ Ⓓ

**11.** Look at the graphic. Where can people register for the tour?

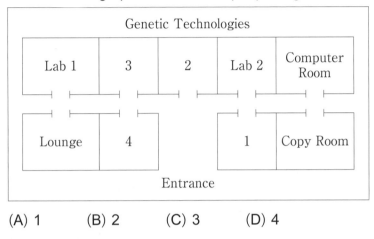

  (A) 1   (B) 2   (C) 3   (D) 4

Ⓐ Ⓑ Ⓒ Ⓓ

**12.** What will take place in the afternoon?
  (A) A discussion about environmental protection
  (B) A talk on genetic research
  (C) A party for the tour group members
  (D) A class on research procedures

Ⓐ Ⓑ Ⓒ Ⓓ

---

### TOEIC 攻略のコツ：[新形式] Parts 3-4　図表問題の対策

Parts 3-4では graphic（図表）を伴うものがありますが、graphic は価格表、時刻表、電話帳、地図、グラフ、メモなどで情報量の少ない単純なものがほとんどです。音声で流れる指示文に内容の種類（announcement, telephone message など）や図表の種類（map, table, sign など）が入るのでこれを聞き取りましょう。解答のヒントになります。（例：Questions 95 through 97 refer to the following announcement and a map.）

# Reading

## 文法問題攻略のポイント：主語と動詞の呼応、時制の一致

1. 動詞の形は主語に呼応するので、主語が単数か複数かを見極めることが重要である。
    例1：Our <u>company</u>, together with other two companies, **has** developed a new medicine.
    例2：The <u>results</u> of the analysis **are** shown in the table.
2. either A or B, neither A nor B, whether A or B, not only A but（also）B, B as well as A, not A but Bのように、AとBが主語になる場合は、Bの数と人称に動詞を呼応させる。
    例：Neither Tom nor <u>John</u> **was** a member of the research group.
3. 一般に主節の動詞が過去時制のときは、次に来る従属節の動詞の時制をこれに合わせて変化させる。
    例：He <u>decided</u> that the experiment **had been** a failure.

## Part 5 Incomplete Sentences

*A word or phrase is missing in each sentence. Choose the best answer to complete the sentence.*

13. Prof. Mason, along with his colleagues, ____ conducted the survey.
    (A) was
    (B) were
    (C) has
    (D) have

14. The results indicated that substance ____ the body seriously.
    (A) affect
    (B) affecting
    (C) have affected
    (D) affected

15. The government as well as private companies _____ in the research project.
    (A) involve
    (B) involved
    (C) is involved
    (D) are involved

16. When you _____ the experiment, clean all the instruments and put them away.
    (A) finish
    (B) will finish
    (C) finished
    (D) are finished

# Part 6 Text Completion

*Read the following text. A word, phrase, or sentence is missing. Choose the best answer to complete the text.*

*Questions 17-19 refer to the following web advertisement.*

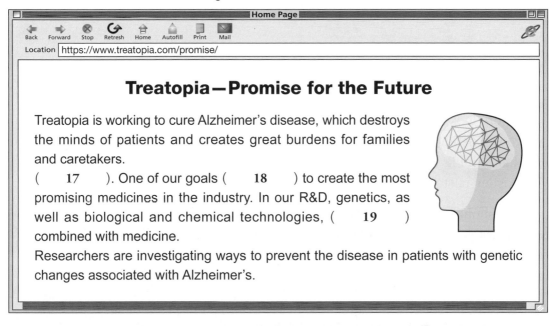

17. (A) All drug companies are working together to develop new medicines.
    (B) No drug companies have been able to slow down the development of the disease so far.
    (C) Drug industries are regulated by the government so that they are not too competitive.
    (D) The drug industry is developing hundreds of medicines for the disease.

18. (A) is  (B) are  (C) were  (D) was

19. (A) had  (B) have  (C) is  (D) are

# Part 7 Reading Comprehension (Single Passages)

*Read the following texts. Each text or set of texts is followed by several questions. Choose the best answer to each question.*

*Questions 20-22 refer to the following Web information.*

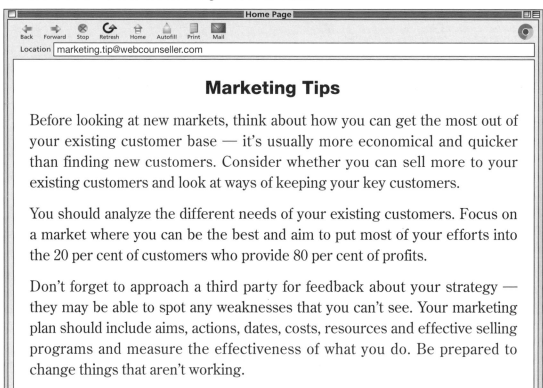

20. What is the main topic of this webpage?
 (A) Advertisement cost
 (B) After-sales service
 (C) Sales strategies
 (D) Annual marketing plan

Ⓐ Ⓑ Ⓒ Ⓓ

21. What marketing advice is given?
 (A) You should comcentrate on your best customers.
 (B) You should try to find new customers.
 (C) You should focus on the top 80 percent of customers.
 (D) You should aim for a 20 percent market share.

Ⓐ Ⓑ Ⓒ Ⓓ

22. What does this webpage recommend you do?
   (A) Not change your plan easily
   (B) Always check other websites
   (C) Think about your situation globally
   (D) Take some advice from a third person

Questions 23-24 refer to the following Web information.

## AI Security

AI's ability to change and remake entire industries is a key driver of investment. In fact, it has led to the creation of entirely new industries. —[1]— In the AI industry, as with many other sectors, cyber security must be a key concern. Generally, people have confidence in AI's effectiveness against cyber-attacks. However, some have warned that relying on AI could increase the chance of information leakage and unauthorized access to confidential data.

As investment continues, there is a need for stricter rules concerning AI and cyber security. —[2]— The regulations under consideration will make it difficult for companies to gather and process user data for their businesses. —[3]— Once the regulations come into effect, companies will need to manage and store their data in a compliant manner.

However, though companies will need to remain compliant with cyber security regulations in our country, AI itself will require many specific laws. —[4]— The industry is making its own regulations and every company in the field has a strong belief in the need for self-regulation about the impacts of AI.

23. What is a problem with the AI security?
   (A) It is very expensive.
   (B) You cannot invest a large amount.
   (C) Your personal data may be leaked.
   (D) You cannot access some important information.

24. In which of the positions marked [1], [2], [3], and [4] does the following sentence best belong?

"But the rewards of investment may carry considerable risks."

(A) [1]   (B) [2]   (C) [3]   (D) [4]

Ⓐ Ⓑ Ⓒ Ⓓ

# Expand your vocabulary! —カタカナ英語や和製英語に注意しましょう！

➢ **claim** 動主張する 名主張（「クレームをつける」は complain）
➢ **mansion** 名大邸宅（「マンション」は condominium）
➢ **plastic bag** ビニール袋
➢ **reform** 動（社会制度・事態などを）改革する（（家などを）改築するは renovate）
➢ **service station** 名ガソリンスタンド（他に gas station/filling station とも言う）
➢ **sign** 名印・合図・掲示 動署名する（「サイン・署名」は signature/autograph）
➢ **smart** 形頭の良い（「ほっそりした」は slender/slim）
➢ **talent** 名才能（「テレビタレント」は TV personality）

# Learn more! — Vocabulary in Context

*Complete each English sentence according to its Japanese translation. The first letter is given.*

1. We need (a          ) data based on careful (o          ).
   （注意深い観察に基づく正確なデータが必要だ。）

2. We've (a          ) AI (t          ) to our office work management.
   （当社は事務管理に人工知能技術を応用しています。）

3. The results of the study (i          ) that it is difficult to find an (o          )
   (s          ).
   （研究の結果は、明白な解決策を見つけるのは難しいことを示唆している。）

4. We have (a          ) a new production method to (m          ) the heavy
   (d          ) of the world market.
   （我が社は、世界市場の大量の需要に応えるために新しい生産方式を採用しました。）

---

1. accurate / observation  2. applied / technology  3. imply / obvious / solution
4. adopted / meet / demand

# Unit 8
## Computers & Technology

21世紀は科学技術の世紀といわれて久しく、現在ではAI（人工知能）や電子マネーやコンピュータを初めとするテクノロジーが私たちの生活の様々な面に入り込んでいます。

## ■ Vocabulary *Match each English word with its meaning in Japanese.* 1-86

| | | |
|---|---|---|
| 1. accelerate ( ) | 2. alternative ( ) | 3. characteristic ( ) |
| 4. copper ( ) | 5. crash ( ) | 6. electromagnet ( ) |
| 7. environment ( ) | 8. era ( ) | 9. exhaust ( ) |
| 10. guideway ( ) | 11. levitation ( ) | 12. nuisance ( ) |
| 13. regenerative ( ) | 14. repel ( ) | 15. upgrade ( ) |

**a.** 加速する　　**b.** 代わりの・選択肢　　**c.** 環境　　**d.** 軌道・案内路　　**e.** 更新する
**f.** 再生する・改造する　　**g.** 時代　　**h.** 銅　　**i.** 特質・独特の　　**j.** 電磁石
**k.** 排気ガス・へとへとに疲れさせる　　**l.** はじく・はね返す
**m.** 不快なこと・やっかいな行為　　**n.** 不作動・衝突・衝突する　　**o.** 浮揚・浮上

## ■ Word Pairs *Fill in each blank to complete the sentences.*

1. In order to (　　　　) the (　　　　　), we should drive more fuel-efficient cars.

2. It has long been said that we have (　　　　　) the (　　　　) of sustainable development.

3. Developing (　　　　)(　　　　　) will contribute to curing a lot of diseases and injuries.

4. Our company is seeking (　　　　)(　　　　) sources.

5. Diesel vehicles may (　　　　　) a lot of poisonous (　　　　　).

| | | |
|---|---|---|
| **a.** alternative / energy | **b.** entered / era | **c.** emit / exhaust |
| **d.** regenerative / cells | **e.** preserve / environment | |

# ■ Listening

## Listening Skill：トピックが何なのかを把握しよう！

リスニングでは、話し手が何について話しているのか、つまりトピックをいくつかのキーワードやキーフレーズから素早く把握することが最も大切です。キーワードは、導入部に置かれることが多いので注意が必要ですが、たとえ導入部を聞き逃しても繰り返し出てくることが多いので最後まで注意して聞きましょう。

## Example 1-87

*You'll hear one conversation with three people and read one question followed by four answers. Fill in the blanks and choose the best answer to the question.*

**Man**: Mary, I've found a few (　　　) in this (　　　) program.
**Woman 1**: Oh, I'm sorry. Shall I rewrite it now?
**Man**: Yes, please. You know such (　　　) might cause a (　　　).
**Woman 1**: Actually, I'm working on making these documents now. Lieu, will you (　　　) this program for Mark?
**Woman 2**: Rely on me, Mary. It's a piece of cake. Mark, can I (　　　) these instructions on the (　　　) first?
**Man**: No problem. But remember, we don't have much time available.

**Question**: What are they talking about?
(A) An insect on the computer
(B) A problem in the computer system
(C) Preparing for a party
(D) Hiring a programmer          Ⓐ Ⓑ Ⓒ Ⓓ

## Part 1  Photographs

*You'll see a picture and hear four short statements. Choose the statement that best describes what you see in the picture.*

**1**

Ⓐ Ⓑ Ⓒ Ⓓ

**2**

Ⓐ Ⓑ Ⓒ Ⓓ

# Part 2 Question - Response  (CD)1-90,91,92,93

*You'll hear a question followed by three responses. Choose the best response to each question.*

3. Mark your answer on your answer sheet.  Ⓐ Ⓑ Ⓒ

4. Mark your answer on your answer sheet.  Ⓐ Ⓑ Ⓒ

5. Mark your answer on your answer sheet.  Ⓐ Ⓑ Ⓒ

6. Mark your answer on your answer sheet.  Ⓐ Ⓑ Ⓒ


# Part 3 Conversation  (CD)1-94,95

*You'll hear one conversation between two people and read three questions followed by four answers. Choose the best answer to each question.*

7. What kind of job will the woman do?
　(A) Software developer
　(B) Systems engineer
　(C) Electrical engineer
　(D) Insurance salesperson

Ⓐ Ⓑ Ⓒ Ⓓ

8. Where will the woman work?
　(A) At a bank
　(B) At a university
　(C) At an insurance company
　(D) At a software company

Ⓐ Ⓑ Ⓒ Ⓓ

9. When will the woman start her new job?
　(A) In March
　(B) In April
　(C) In June
　(D) In September

Ⓐ Ⓑ Ⓒ Ⓓ

# Part 4 Talk ((CD))1-96,97

*You'll hear one talk and read three questions about the talk. The questions will be followed by four answers. Choose the best answer to each question.*

10. How much will Internet Systems pay for MyFace?
   (A) 30 million dollars
   (B) 90 million dollars
   (C) 300 million dollars
   (D) 900 million dollars

   Ⓐ Ⓑ Ⓒ Ⓓ

11. What kind of company is MyFace?
   (A) An Internet sales company
   (B) An Internet provider
   (C) An Internet advertising company
   (D) An Internet friendship site

   Ⓐ Ⓑ Ⓒ Ⓓ

12. What Internet users does Internet Systems hope to attract?
   (A) Business users
   (B) Young users
   (C) Internet experts
   (D) Elderly users

   Ⓐ Ⓑ Ⓒ Ⓓ

---

## TOEIC 攻略のコツ：[新形式] Part 3　会話問題の対策

新形式では、従来の2人の会話に加え3人の会話についての設問が出題されます。指示文で "Questions X-Y refer to the following conversation with three speakers" と聞こえたら3人の会話であると判断しましょう。男性2人＋女性1人または男性1人＋女性2人の場合があります。同性の2人が話す英語は違っている場合（アメリカ英語、イギリス英語、オーストラリア英語など）が多いので、普段から様々な英語を聞いておくとよいでしょう。質問は Wh 疑問文がほとんどなので、「誰が、いつ、どこで、何を、どうして」などを聴き取りましょう。また、新形式問題では、wanna や gonna などの省略形や主語や動詞などが抜けている不完全な文が含まれるようになり、会話がより自然になったことも覚えておきましょう。

# Reading

## 文法問題攻略のポイント：能動態＆受動態

1. 受動態の作り方：目的語を主語に変え be 動詞 + p. p.（+ by ...）を用いる。
    例 1：The computer processes more and more data.（SVO）→ More and more data **are processed** by the computer.
    例 2：A stranger sent her an e-mail.（SVOO）→ She **was sent** an e-mail by a stranger. / An e-mail **was sent**（**to**）her by a stranger.
    例 3：We cannot leave the machine running.（SVOC）→ The machine cannot **be left** running.
2. 一般に say, think, suppose, believe, consider, etc. + that 節の文からは２つの受動態ができる。
    例：People say that the U. S. entered a new era of technology. → **It is said that** the U. S. entered a new era of technology. / The U. S. **is said to** have entered a new era of technology.
3. 一般に surprised, amazed, frightened, delighted, disappointed, satisfied, covered, known などは形容詞とみなされ、by 以外の前置詞を伴うことが多い。
    例：I **was surprised at** the innovations in renewable energy.
4. laugh at, look up to, take advantage of などの句動詞を受動態にするときには、前置詞を落とさないように注意！
    例 1：We **were called on** by a computer engineer yesterday.
    例 2：These animals must **be taken good care of**.

## Part 5 Incomplete Sentences

*A word or phrase is missing in each sentence. Choose the best answer to complete the sentence.*

13. Our laboratory is ____ in the State of Maine, which has a rich natural environment.
    (A) locate        (C) locating
    (B) located       (D) location
    Ⓐ Ⓑ Ⓒ Ⓓ

14. Did I tell you I ____ married on Aug. 5th? My husband's name is Richard Gordon and he is a computer programmer.
    (A) am    (B) did    (C) got    (D) was
    Ⓐ Ⓑ Ⓒ Ⓓ

15. I regret to say that the product we received today ____ damaged.
    (A) is        (C) has
    (B) were      (D) had
    Ⓐ Ⓑ Ⓒ Ⓓ

16. Last year I hoped more public attention ____ to our new technology.
    (A) will pay          (C) would have paid
    (B) would be paying   (D) would be paid
    Ⓐ Ⓑ Ⓒ Ⓓ

# Part 6 Text Completion

*Read the following text. A word, phrase, or sentence is missing. Choose the best answer to complete the text.*

*Questions 17-19 refer to the following web advertisement.*

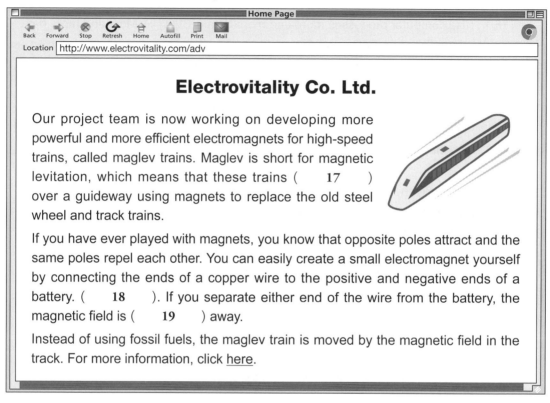

17. (A) have floated (B) will float (C) to float (D) floated

18. (A) This generates a lot of electricity.
    (B) This results in freezing the track.
    (C) This contributes to the field research.
    (D) This creates a small magnetic field.

19. (A) take (B) took (C) taken (D) taking

# Part 7 Reading Comprehension (Double Passages)

*Read the following texts. Each text or set of texts is followed by several questions. Choose the best answer to each question.*

*Questions 20-24 refer to the following question and answer on a webpage.*

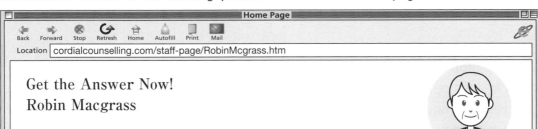

Location: cordialcounselling.com/staff-page/RobinMcgrass.htm

Get the Answer Now!
Robin Macgrass

Hi Robin,

I'm Hugo Sanchez from San Diego, C.A. For over a year, I've been deeply impressed by your opinions and suggestions in "Get the Answer Now!" My problem is that I spent too much time on social networking sites. Half a year ago I signed up with a leading SNS because it was a handy way of sharing vacation photos with my family and friends. But now, things are getting out of hand. I've made many online friends recently. Like most people, I keep in touch with some of them regularly, while others are simply on my Christmas card list. In this way, I spend way too much time getting posts from some people saying "Hey, Hugo, I haven't seen you since we were in college. Where have you been hiding for the last 20 years?" Then others text me a lot of pictures. With some people, it's a nuisance. What shall I do with these guys?

Hi Hugo,

I'm concerned about your message and suppose that many others have the same kind of problems. Of course, it may be amazing how many long-lost pals seem to appear when you join an SNS. However, one or two of your old friends saw you on the SNS, word spread quickly, and you're reconnecting with all sorts of people from the past. All of this shows that digital exhaustion is a serious problem which many of you don't know how to cope with. It's still such a steep digital learning curve that you should limit the time you spend dealing with your SNS and check for incoming messages just a couple of times a day. Maybe the best answer is to return to the days of handwritten letters.

20. What does Robin Macgrass do?
   (A) Newscaster
   (B) Advice columnist
   (C) Police officer
   (D) Teacher

   Ⓐ Ⓑ Ⓒ Ⓓ

21. What problem does Hugo have?
   (A) He does not have enough time to deal with SNS.
   (B) He does not have any friends on SNS.
   (C) He cannot understand how to get access to SNS.
   (D) His friends deleted his information on SNS.

   Ⓐ Ⓑ Ⓒ Ⓓ

22. What is the possible reason Robin took up Hugo's inquiry?
   (A) He thought that it would be a common problem among elderly people.
   (B) He thought that it was a good example of someone's coping with his or her friends properly.
   (C) He thought that it would be the worst problem someone might have.
   (D) He thought that it could be shared by many other people.

   Ⓐ Ⓑ Ⓒ Ⓓ

23. According to Robin, what is a problem that SNS users may face?
   (A) They may be involved in unnecessary arguments.
   (B) They may encounter strangers including criminals.
   (C) They may get tired of chatting with unwanted people.
   (D) They may spend too much money on SNS.

   Ⓐ Ⓑ Ⓒ Ⓓ

24. What is one of Robin's solutions for Hugo?
   (A) He should block his friends from SNS.
   (B) He should stop using SNS.
   (C) He should spend less time using SNS.
   (D) He should meet his friends in person without using SNS.

   Ⓐ Ⓑ Ⓒ Ⓓ

· · · · · · · · · · · · · · · · · · · · · ·

# Expand your vocabulary! —同音異義語に注意！

➤ **council** 名評議会 / **counsel** 名助言・相談 動助言する・勧める
➤ **flower** 名 / **flour** 名小麦粉
➤ **lesson** 名学課・授業・教訓 / **lessen** 動少なくする・小さくする
➤ **mail** 名郵便 / **male** 名男性・男子 形男性の
➤ **principal** 形主な・主要な / **principle** 名校長・社長
➤ **cite** 動引用する / **sight** 名視力・光景 動見つける / **site** 名場所
➤ **waist** 名（人体の）ウエスト / **waste** 動浪費する・無駄にする 名浪費・廃棄物
➤ **way** 名道・方向・方法 / **weigh** 動重さが…ある・重さを量る

# Learn more! — Vocabulary in Context

*Complete each English sentence according to its Japanese translation. The first letter is given.*

1. The design you provided is technically good, but does not (f          )
   (i     )(w       ) our strategic goals.
   （あなたの提出したデザインは技術的にはよくできていますが、我が社の戦略目標と合っていません。）

2. Choose the calling plan most (s       )(f       ) your mobile needs.
   （あなたの携帯電話需要に最も適した通話料金プランを選びなさい。）

3. Because of the time required to change the program, I feel it is wise to
   (l       ) it as it is for the (t       )(b       ).
   （プログラムの変更には時間がかかるので、今のところそれはそのままにしておいた方が賢明だと思います。）

4. The business world in Asia is highly dynamic and the spread of telecommunications is (a       ) the (r       ) of change.
   （アジアのビジネス界は非常に活動的で、遠距離通信手段の拡大により、変化のスピードが加速化しています。）

---

1. fit / in / with  2. suitable / for  3. leave / time / being  4. accelerating / rate

77

# Unit 9
## Employment & Promotions

このユニットでは、求職・就職・昇進・転職・退職を主題として扱います。現在では求職・転職の手段としてウェブ検索が欠かせません。さらに会社や団体との連絡にはＥメールやＳＮＳも頻繁に使われています。

## ■ Vocabulary  *Match each English word with its meaning in Japanese.* 2-01

| | | |
|---|---|---|
| 1. accountant ( ) | 2. alternate ( ) | 3. ambitious ( ) |
| 4. bachelor ( ) | 5. description ( ) | 6. farewell ( ) |
| 7. opportunity ( ) | 8. promote ( ) | 9. register ( ) |
| 10. representative ( ) | 11. resignation ( ) | 12. résumé ( ) |
| 13. reward ( ) | 14. sociable ( ) | 15. submit ( ) |

a. 会計士・会計係　　b. 学士　　c. 価値がある・報酬　　d. 機会　　e. 記述・描写
f. 交互の・1つおきの　　g. 辞職　　h. 社交的な・交際上手な
i. 昇進させる・促進する　　j. 代表者・代理人・代表する　　k. 提出する
l. 登録する・名簿　　m. 野心のある・熱望して　　n. 履歴書　　o. 別れ

## ■ Word Pairs  *Fill in each blank to complete the sentences.*

1. Scandinavian nations are proud of their high social benefits and low ( )
   ( ) due to work-sharing.

2. My friend is attending business school to be a ( )( ).

3. I have to ( ) my ( ) to that organization as soon as possible.

4. In order to apply for this position, you are required to have a master's degree,
   not just a ( )( ).

5. She's been taking qualifying exams to ( ) her ( ).

| | | |
|---|---|---|
| a. bachelor's / degree | b. advance / career | c. registered / accountant |
| d. submit / résumés | e. unemployment / rate | |

78

# Listening

## Listening Skill：会話や説明文の状況・場所・人間関係を把握しよう！

リスニングにおいては、話し手のいる場所や人間関係などを聞き取ることが大切です。キーワードからこれらの状況をできるだけ早く聞き取ることがリスニング上達の秘訣です。

## Example 2-02

*You'll hear one conversation between two people and read one question followed by four answers. Fill in the blanks and choose the best answer to the question.*

**Man**: Hi, Lee.
**Woman**: Hi, Mark. What's up?
**Man**: I just heard about your (          ) to manager of the (          ) division.
**Woman**: Oh, yes.
**Man**: Congratulations!
**Woman**: Thank you.
**Man**: I know you got a registered (          ) license recently, so you must be very happy with your (          )(          ).
**Woman**: Yes, I am. Thanks a lot.

**Question**: What has happened to Lee?
 (A) She has begun to work as an accountant lately.
 (B) She has become head of the personnel department.
 (C) She has got promoted to head of the accounting department.
 (D) She has congratulated the man.          Ⓐ Ⓑ Ⓒ Ⓓ

## Part 1 Photographs

*You'll see a picture and hear four short statements. Choose the statement that best describes what you see in the picture.*

**1**

Ⓐ Ⓑ Ⓒ Ⓓ

**2**

Ⓐ Ⓑ Ⓒ Ⓓ

# Part 2  Question - Response  2-05,06,07,08

*You'll hear a question followed by three responses. Choose the best response to each question.*

3. Mark your answer on your answer sheet.  Ⓐ Ⓑ Ⓒ

4. Mark your answer on your answer sheet.  Ⓐ Ⓑ Ⓒ

5. Mark your answer on your answer sheet.  Ⓐ Ⓑ Ⓒ

6. Mark your answer on your answer sheet.  Ⓐ Ⓑ Ⓒ


# Part 3  Conversation  2-09,10

*You'll hear one conversation between two people and read three questions followed by four answers. Choose the best answer to each question.*

7. When is the man going to Tokyo?
  (A) In January
  (B) In February
  (C) A year from now
  (D) A week from now

  Ⓐ Ⓑ Ⓒ Ⓓ


8. What department will the man work in in Tokyo?
  (A) In the marketing department
  (B) In the advertising department
  (C) In the accounting department
  (D) In the operations department

  Ⓐ Ⓑ Ⓒ Ⓓ


9. How does the woman think the man will feel about working in Japan?
  (A) He will miss his home.
  (B) He will be very busy.
  (C) He will not enjoy it.
  (D) He will like it.

  Ⓐ Ⓑ Ⓒ Ⓓ

# Part 4 Talk 2-11,12

*You'll hear one talk and read three questions about the talk. The questions will be followed by four answers. Choose the best answer to each question.*

10. Who most likely are the listeners?
   (A) Journalists
   (B) University students
   (C) Employers
   (D) University professors

   (A)(B)(C)(D)

11. What advice can listeners receive?
   (A) How to dress for business
   (B) How to become a representative
   (C) How to behave at an interview
   (D) How to negotiate salary

   (A)(B)(C)(D)

12. What does the speaker imply when he says, "We have a large crowd here this year, so be sure to register for your interviews"?
   (A) The speaker is disappointed by the size of the audience.
   (B) Arranging an interview will be easy.
   (C) The speaker wishes fewer people had come to the event.
   (D) The number of interview openings is limited.

   (A)(B)(C)(D)

---

## TOEIC 攻略のコツ：Parts 5-7　時間配分に気を付けよう

TOEIC は時間との戦いです。Listening Parts 1-4 にかかる約45分の時間を除くと、残り約75分の間に Reading Parts 5-7 の全100問を解くことになります。Parts 5-6 は、ほぼ文法と語法（look for..., ability to do など）や語彙なので1問最長でも30秒で解答し、余った時間は Part 6 の文挿入問題と Part 7 などに使い、これらの設問も1問約1分程度で解答しましょう。それぞれの設問が制限時間内に終わらない場合は、恐らく後で見直ししている時間はないため、空欄を作らず最も適切だと思われる選択肢にマークして次に進みましょう。

---

81

# Reading

## 文法問題攻略のポイント：不定詞＆動名詞

1. 不定詞には3つの用法がある。
    例1：I would like **to work** in the personnel department.（名詞的）
    例2：I welcome anyone **to respond**.（形容詞的）
    例3：I have been studying English **to enjoy** a working holiday in Australia.（副詞的）
2. 特に不定詞を目的語にとる動詞〔expect, hope, want, wish, plan, mean, decide, learn, pretend, agree, etc.〕に注意！
    例：I <u>plan</u> **to study** in Britain after making enough money at this firm.
3. 不定詞を使った慣用詞にも注意！
    例：**To tell** <u>the truth</u>, I need advice on how to find a job in Canada.
4. 一般に動名詞は文の主語・補語・動詞や前置詞の目的語になるとともに、それ自体が意味上の主語や目的語・補語などを伴うことができる。
    例1：**Being** on time is my usual habit.（主語）
    例2：My hobbies are **playing** tennis, **skiing** and **climbing** mountains.（補語）
    例3：I am concerned about your **losing** job opportunities.（前置詞の目的語）
5. 特に動名詞を目的語にとる(句)動詞〔mind, miss, enjoy, give up, avoid, finish, escape, put off, postpone, stop, dislike, deny, admit, etc.〕に注意！
    例：Do you <u>mind</u> **coming** to see us at 10:00 a.m. next Saturday?
6. 動名詞の慣用句は数が多いので注意！
    例：On <u>hearing</u> my brother was accepted by the company, I <u>could not help</u> **crying**.

## Part 5 Incomplete Sentences

*A word or phrase is missing in each sentence. Choose the best answer to complete the sentence.*

13. We have decided _____ in two contractors for the project.
    (A) bring          (C) to bring
    (B) brought        (D) bringing
    Ⓐ Ⓑ Ⓒ Ⓓ

14. I tried to persuade Tom _____ for the job, but he refused.
    (A) to apply       (C) applied
    (B) apply          (D) applying
    Ⓐ Ⓑ Ⓒ Ⓓ

15. I apologize for not _____ into contact with you sooner.
    (A) to get         (C) getting
    (B) have gotten    (D) to have gotten
    Ⓐ Ⓑ Ⓒ Ⓓ

16. Kenny took full responsibility for the scandal _____ in his resignation.
    (A) to hand        (C) by handing
    (B) handed         (D) to have handed
    Ⓐ Ⓑ Ⓒ Ⓓ

# Part 6 Text Completion

*Read the following text. A word, phrase, or sentence is missing. Choose the best answer to complete the text.*

*Questions 17-19 refer to the following letter.*

---

December 5, 20XX
Ideal Metals, Ltd.

Ladies and gentlemen:
I am writing to let you know that due to a health problem I am determined (    17    ) to Greece and that a new office manager will be sent in my place. Until the arrival of the new manager, Mr. Arhan Sanghera will be acting in that position.

I am very grateful for the cooperation I have received from you and your colleagues in the short time that I have been in Canada. I would hope that you will extend the same cooperation to Mr. Sanghera and to my successor when he or she arrives.

(    18    ) However, I regret (    19    ) that illness has prevented me from calling on you personally and making my farewells.
Yours sincerely,

*Mikis Andronicus*
Mikis Andronicus
Manager

---

17. (A) return    (B) returning    (C) to return    (D) returned

Ⓐ Ⓑ Ⓒ Ⓓ

18. (A) Indeed I want to vacate my seat for you.
    (B) Of course, I am eager to talk face to face with you again.
    (C) Needless to say, I want to apologize to you for my misconduct.
    (D) It goes without saying that I have wanted to quit my position.

Ⓐ Ⓑ Ⓒ Ⓓ

19. (A) say    (B) saying    (C) to say    (D) said

Ⓐ Ⓑ Ⓒ Ⓓ

# Part 7 Reading Comprehension (Single Passages)

Read the following texts. Each text or set of texts is followed by several questions. Choose the best answer to each question.

*Questions 20-21 refer to the following letter.*

Ms. Juliette von Arthur
Executive Managing Director
Arthur, Kates & Associates
1873 West 17th Street
Chicago, IL 60611
U. S. A.

Hello Juliette,

Just a line to let you know that Lily and I have been well. We are both working hard and doing lots of traveling. We are leaving for New Zealand on the 15th.

One of my clients, a British woman, is interested in working in the U.S.A. She received her Master's degree in the field of transportation and wrote her thesis on problems in American subway system. Hanna Williams is 25 years old and quite sociable. If you don't mind, I will have her send you a description of her background and capabilities.

Hope you and your family are doing well.

Lily & Margaret

20. What is the relationship between Juliette and Margaret?
(A) Travel agent and client
(B) Friends
(C) Teacher and student
(D) Manager and worker

ⒶⒷⒸⒹ

21. Why will Hanna Williams come to the U.S.A.?
(A) She will seek employment.
(B) She will go sightseeing.
(C) She will be in transit.
(D) She will study.

ⒶⒷⒸⒹ

84

*Questions 22-24 refer to the following message chain.*

---

**Vincent, Carl** [9:10 A.M.]
Good morning and welcome, Ms. Kathy Donovan. I'm manager at Michigan Brainwork's head office. Mary Kenneth will take you under her wing and give you a more complete rundown of your responsibilities.

**Donovan, Kathy** [9:12 A.M.]
Thank you, Carl. It's a real pleasure to have this opportunity to work with you at headquarters next Monday. I'll try my best to be a good team player.

**Kenneth, Mary** [9:13 A.M.]
Welcome aboard, Kathy. I'm Mary, the assistant manager. Please don't hesitate to ask me any questions.

**Vincent, Carl** [9:15 A.M.]
Speak of the devil, here she is. Mary, will you give Kathy more details about what she should do?

**Kenneth, Mary** [9:16 A.M.]
Certainly. But I'm a nice devil. I'm ready to explain to you, Kathy. Your office hours are 9 to 6, Monday through Friday. In the summer months, July-September, though, you can take alternate Fridays off by working an additional hour each day.

**Donovan, Kathy** [9:17 A.M.]
I'm so excited to be working with you, Mary.

**Kenneth, Mary** [9:18 A.M.]
So am I, Kathy. When you arrive at the office next Monday morning, I'll give you the employee handbook, which covers most of the essentials you need to know about working at head office. It includes an updated staff list and organization chart which should help you get the lay of the land here.

**Donovan, Kathy** [9:19 A.M.]
Thank you, Carl and Mary. I'm looking forward to meeting you next week.

**Kenneth, Mary** [9:21 A.M.]
See you next Monday.

**Vincent, Carl** [9:23 A.M.]
See you then.

---

22. What is Kathy Donovan's situation?
    (A) New part-time employee at the company
    (B) New full-time worker at head office
    (C) New assistant manager at a branch office
    (D) New manager at the headquarters         Ⓐ Ⓑ Ⓒ Ⓓ

23. At 9:15 A.M., what does Carl mean when he says, "Speak of the devil"?
    (A) He thinks Mary might interfere with their conversation.
    (B) He is angry at Mary because she is late.
    (C) He probably wants to avoid talking with Mary.
    (D) He probably wants to break the ice by making a joke.         Ⓐ Ⓑ Ⓒ Ⓓ

**24.** Which is part of Kathy Donovan's working conditions?

  (A) She has to work part-time for the time being.

  (B) She has to work longer in July-September than the other months.

  (C) She can have longer off-days in the summertime.

  (D) She has to work on Fridays in the summertime.     Ⓐ Ⓑ Ⓒ Ⓓ

# Expand your vocabulary! ―同義語句を調べよう。

➤ **bring about**（…をもたらす）= cause, result in

➤ **call off**（…を中止する）= cancel, set aside

➤ **come across**（…とばったり出会う）= run into, encounter

➤ **deal with**（…を扱う）= cope with, treat

➤ **do away with**（…を廃止する）= abolish

➤ **get to**（…に着く）= arrive at / in, reach

➤ **give up**（…をやめる）= abandon, stop

➤ **like**（…を好む）= be fond of, care for

➤ **look after**（…の世話をする）= take care of, nurse

➤ **put off**（…を延期する）= postpone, delay

➤ **take after**（…と似ている）= resemble, look like

# Learn more! ― Vocabulary in Context

*Complete each English sentence according to its Japanese translation. The first letter is given.*

**1.** Long lines of out-of-work people waited patiently to (s        )(u        ) (f      ) their unemployment benefits.

  （失業給付金の登録をするために、失業者が長蛇の列を作って辛抱強く待っていた。）

**2.** Job (o        ) for adults fell by just over 1,000 to 227,000 during the period (u       )(r       ).

  （調査期間中に成年の求人は1,000人強減少し、227,000人になった。）

**3.** Two-year (r        )(c        ) begin on September 1st this year. The salary is highly (c       ) and related to qualifications and experience.

  （更新可能な2年契約が、本年9月1日より始まります。給与は他社と十分に競合できるものですし、資格と経験に応じて優遇いたします。）

**4.** Please mail, fax or email a cover letter, a (r        ), and the names of three (r       ) to the personnel department.

  （郵便かファクスかEメールで、カバーレター、履歴書、3名の推薦者のお名前を人事部までお送りください。）

---

1. sign/up/for  2. opportunities/under/review  3. renewable/contracts/competitive  4. résumé/references

# Unit 10
## Advertisements & Personnel

私たちは様々な宣伝や広告から情報を得ています。現在ではウェブや SNS などを通じた広告も一般的です。このユニットでは、会社や団体の人材募集や製品の宣伝や広告などについて学びましょう。

## ■ Vocabulary  *Match each English word with its meaning in Japanese.* 🎧2-13

| | | |
|---|---|---|
| 1. adopt ( ) | 2. agency ( ) | 3. applicant ( ) |
| 4. classified ( ) | 5. commodity ( ) | 6. device ( ) |
| 7. enthusiastic ( ) | 8. interpersonal ( ) | 9. massive ( ) |
| 10. mechanical ( ) | 11. promotional ( ) | 12. qualification ( ) |
| 13. recruit ( ) | 14. requirement ( ) | 15. vacancy ( ) |

a. 空き・欠員・空室　　b. 案内広告の・分類された　　c. 応募者　　d. 機械の・機械的な

e. 採用する　　f. 資格・能力　　g. 商品　　h. 新人・募集する　　i. 装置

j. 大規模の・大きい　　k. 対人関係の　　l. 代理店・仲介・政府機関

m. 熱心な・熱中して　　n. 販売促進の　　o. 必要条件・要件

## ■ Word Pairs  *Fill in each blank to complete the sentences.*

1. (　　　　　)(　　　　　　　) can be found in newspapers, online and in other periodicals.

2. We have launched a massive (　　　　)(　　　　　) campaign to sell the washing machines.

3. That company boasts of maintaining its (　　　　　)(　　　　　) system.

4. We must employ more workers to make up for our current (　　　　　) (　　　　　).

5. We have (　　　　　) a 4-day (　　　　　) so that our employees have time to take care of their family.

a. public / relations　　b. classified / advertisements　　c. lifetime / employment

d. adopted / workweek　e. labor / shortage

# ■ Listening

## Listening Skill：場面をイメージしよう！

英語を聞きながら頭の中で和訳をしてはいけません。翻訳には時間がかかり、そうしているうちに話は先に進行してしまっているからです。そこで house が聞こえたら「家」と翻訳しないで🏠を、move to a new house が聞こえたら具体的に自分が新居に引っ越している場面をイメージしましょう。

## Example  2-14

*Look at the price list. You'll hear one conversation between two people and read one questions followed by four answers. Fill in the blanks and choose the best answer to the question.*

**Back-to-School Sale**
**Rainbow Stationery Center**

Stapler……$4.00
Scissors……$3.00
Mechanical pencil……$3.00
Felt-tip pen……$1.00
Loose-leaf binder……$2.00

**Woman**: Can I help you, sir?
**Man**: Yes, please. I received a direct mail from your store, and found mechanical pencils and felt-tip pens are (　　　)(　　　).
**Woman**: We're very sorry, sir. Felt-tip pens have already (　　　)(　　　). We can provide you with ball-point pens at the (　　　)(　　　), instead.
**Man**: OK. Then give me one mechanical pencil and one black ball-point pen.

**Question**: Look at the graphic. How much will the man pay?
(A) One dollar　(B) Three dollars　(C) Four dollars　(D) Five dollars

Ⓐ Ⓑ Ⓒ Ⓓ

## Part 1 Photographs

*You'll see a picture and hear four short statements. Choose the statement that best describes what you see in the picture.*

**1**  2-15

Ⓐ Ⓑ Ⓒ Ⓓ

**2**  2-16

Ⓐ Ⓑ Ⓒ Ⓓ

# Part 2 Question - Response (CD)2-17,18,19,20

*You'll hear a question followed by three responses. Choose the best response to each question.*

3. Mark your answer on your answer sheet. Ⓐ Ⓑ Ⓒ

4. Mark your answer on your answer sheet. Ⓐ Ⓑ Ⓒ

5. Mark your answer on your answer sheet. Ⓐ Ⓑ Ⓒ

6. Mark your answer on your answer sheet. Ⓐ Ⓑ Ⓒ

# Part 3 Conversation (CD)2-21,22

*You'll hear one conversation between two people and read three questions followed by four answers. Choose the best answer to each question.*

7. What kind of company do the man and woman work for?
   (A) A travel agency
   (B) A sports equipment company
   (C) An airline
   (D) An advertising agency

Ⓐ Ⓑ Ⓒ Ⓓ

8. Look at the graphic. What activities will the campaign focus on?

| Most Popular Outdoor Activities | | | |
|---|---|---|---|
| 1 | Snorkeling | 5 | Mountain biking |
| 2 | Whale watching | 6 | Horseback riding |
| 3 | Hiking | 7 | Helicopter ride |
| 4 | Golf | 8 | Birdwatching |

   (A) All eight activities
   (B) Snorkeling, whale watching, and hiking
   (C) The top five activities
   (D) Snorkeling and whale watching

Ⓐ Ⓑ Ⓒ Ⓓ

9. What is the woman concerned about?
   (A) They do not have enough money to buy televisions.
   (B) Advertising on television is expensive.
   (C) The client cannot afford to pay for magazine advertising.
   (D) She thinks magazine ads are more effective than TV ads.

Ⓐ Ⓑ Ⓒ Ⓓ

# Part 4 Talk 2-23,24

*You'll hear one talk and read three questions about the talk. The questions will be followed by four answers. Choose the best answer to each question.*

10. Which of the following is NOT a requirement for this job?
   (A) Energy
   (B) Imagination
   (C) Interpersonal skills
   (D) Experience

Ⓐ Ⓑ Ⓒ Ⓓ

11. What is mentioned as a good feature of this job?
   (A) Free travel
   (B) Chances for promotion
   (C) Insurance benefits
   (D) Long vacations

Ⓐ Ⓑ Ⓒ Ⓓ

12. When does the next training program begin?
   (A) In eight weeks
   (B) In six weeks
   (C) In April
   (D) In August

Ⓐ Ⓑ Ⓒ Ⓓ

---

## TOEIC 攻略のコツ：Parts 6-7
## Scanning と Skimming の方法を身に付けよう

Parts 6-7の英文読解問題の本文を制限時間内に全部読むのは非常に困難です。そこで必要不可欠なのが scanning と skimming です。scanning は特定の情報を探しながら読む方法で、skimming は全体の内容を素早く理解するための速読法です。Part 7では設問の順序通り本文にヒントが与えられている場合が多いので、まずはキーワードから scanning を行なって解ける設問を解き、それで解決できない設問は skimming をして、最初と最後の paragraphs（段落）、さらに各 paragraph の最初の sentence（文）を読んでヒントを見つけましょう。

# Reading

## 文法問題攻略のポイント：分詞

1. 分詞は形容詞的な働きをして名詞の前後に置かれ名詞を修飾する。
   例1：Who is that **sleeping** guy?
   例2：I went to the store to get the **advertised** item.
   例3：We provide services at locations **ranging** from North City to South City.
   例4：I completely agree with the information **provided** to me.
2. 分詞は目的格補語になる。
   例1：The boss saw his employee **sleeping** at the desk.
   例2：The boss had his extra work **finished** by his employee.
3. 分詞は分詞構文として、副詞的に文を修飾し、副詞節を短くして副詞句を作る。一般に、分詞の意味上の主語は主節の主語と同じであるが、違う場合は分詞の前に意味上の主語を置く。
   例1：**Seeing**[When he saw]me at the interview, the director kindly offered me a seat. 様子や状態を表し「〜しながら」「〜して」という意味になる。
   例2：He left the office, just **saying** good-bye.
4. with とともに用いられ様子や状態を表し、前に置かれる名詞句が分詞の意味上の主語となる。
   例：Send your job application form with your photo **enclosed**.

## Part 5 Incomplete Sentences

*A word or phrase is missing in each sentence. Choose the best answer to complete the sentence.*

13. In order to choose the most suitable applicant for the position, you should explain in detail the essential qualifications and experience ____ for the job.
    (A) require     (C) required
    (B) requiring   (D) to require
    Ⓐ Ⓑ Ⓒ Ⓓ

14. ____ full-time, you will be eligible for medical insurance, vacation and holiday pay, and other benefits.
    (A) Work        (C) Worked
    (B) Working     (D) Have worked
    Ⓐ Ⓑ Ⓒ Ⓓ

15. Our members are passionate, engaged people ____ their lives and interests with others.
    (A) shared        (C) to be shared
    (B) sharing       (D) having shared
    Ⓐ Ⓑ Ⓒ Ⓓ

16. Please send your personal history with your picture ____ to it.
    (A) attached      (C) attach
    (B) attaching     (D) to attach
    Ⓐ Ⓑ Ⓒ Ⓓ

# Part 6 Text Completion

*Read the following text. A word, phrase, or sentence is missing. Choose the best answer to complete the text.*

*Questions 17-19 refer to the following web advertisement.*

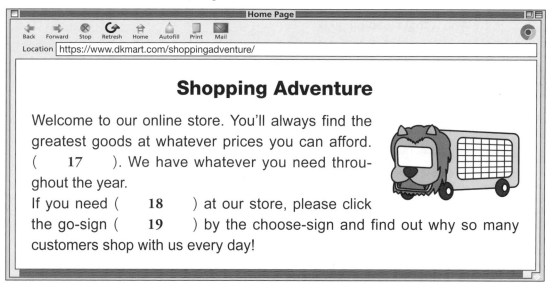

## Shopping Adventure

Welcome to our online store. You'll always find the greatest goods at whatever prices you can afford. (  17  ). We have whatever you need throughout the year.

If you need (  18  ) at our store, please click the go-sign (  19  ) by the choose-sign and find out why so many customers shop with us every day!

17. (A) We can dispatch our staff to any place you live in.
    (B) You can sell whatever you want to at your own price.
    (C) We offer everything ranging from computers to clothes.
    (D) You can visit us seven days a week from 7:00 a.m. to 11:00 p.m.

18. (A) to shop
    (B) shopping
    (C) shop
    (D) to be shopped

19. (A) to follow
    (B) following
    (C) follow
    (D) followed

# Part 7 Reading Comprehension (Single Passages)

Read the following texts. Each text or set of texts is followed by several questions. Choose the best answer to each question.

Questions 20-21 refer to the following web advertisement.

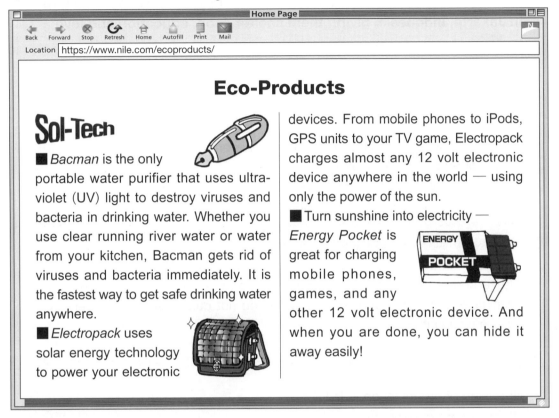

20. What can you do with Bacman?
   (A) Make water safe for drinking
   (B) Keep yourself safe from ultraviolet rays
   (C) Make your driving safer
   (D) Get to your destination easily

21. What is true about both Electropack and Energy Pocket?
   (A) They are small computers powered by solar energy.
   (B) They can be used with all types of batteries.
   (C) They can be used to charge electronic devices.
   (D) They can be used to repair electronic devices.

Questions 22-24 refer to the following Webpage.

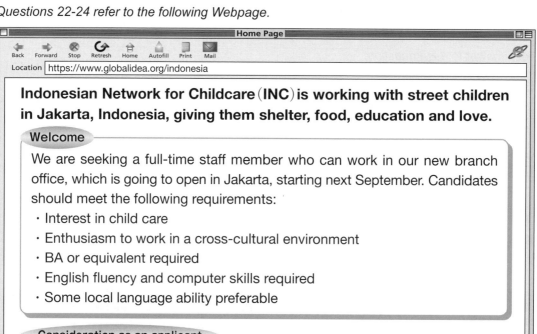

22. What kind of organization is INC?
 (A) It takes care of old people.
 (B) It takes care of poor families.
 (C) It takes care of poor children.
 (D) It takes care of criminals.

23. Which of the following is NOT included in the job requirements?
 (A) Academic background
 (B) Past career
 (C) Language skills
 (D) Desire to work in an international environment

24. Which of the following statements is true?
 (A) People have to submit their official résumé online.
 (B) People must visit the INC office to apply for the post.
 (C) INC will provide people with an application form on the Internet.
 (D) INC must consider every résumé handed in.

Ⓐ Ⓑ Ⓒ Ⓓ

## Expand your vocabulary! ―反意語も一緒に覚えましょう！
➤ **active** ⇔ **passive, inactive**
➤ **agreement** ⇔ **disagreement, discord, misunderstanding**
➤ **dangerous** ⇔ **safe, secure**
➤ **different** ⇔ **similar, alike, identical** (**indifferent** は「無関心で」)
➤ **empty** ⇔ 形**full, filled** / 動**fill**
➤ **expensive** ⇔ **cheap, inexpensive, modest, low-priced, low-cost**
➤ **negative** ⇔ **positive, affirmative**
➤ **physical** ⇔ **mental, spiritual**
➤ **polite** ⇔ **impolite, rude**
➤ **private** ⇔ **public**

## Learn more! ― Vocabulary in Context
*Complete each English sentence according to its Japanese translation. The first letter is given.*

1. Your (a              ) letter does not have to explain your experience (i              )
 (d              ).
 (あなたの応募書類で、あなたの経験を詳細に説明する必要はありません。)

2. I am (a              )(f              ) an interview at your (c              ).
 (ご都合のよろしい時に、面接に応じられます。)

3. The personnel manager had to (a              )(f              ) a (r              )
 immediately.
 (人事部長は急いで代わりの人を手配しなければならなかった。)

4. The number of (v              ) is well above the number of people (s              )
 (e              ).
 (求人数は求職者数を大幅に上回っている。)

---

1. application / in / detail  2. available / for / convenience  3. arrange / for / replacement
4. vacancies / seeking / employment

95

# Unit 11
## Telephone & Messages

このユニットでは、電話やＥメールなどの通信に関するトピックを扱います。ビジネスにおいても欠かせないこれらの通信手段について、英語ではどのように表現するのでしょうか。

## ■ Vocabulary  *Match each English word with its meaning in Japanese.*  2-25

| | | |
|---|---|---|
| 1. appointment ( ) | 2. attachment ( ) | 3. attitude ( ) |
| 4. connect ( ) | 5. extension ( ) | 6. guarantee ( ) |
| 7. inspection ( ) | 8. minimal ( ) | 9. mobile ( ) |
| 10. monthly ( ) | 11. postage ( ) | 12. recharge ( ) |
| 13. spam ( ) | 14. text ( ) | 15. virus ( ) |

**a.** ウイルス　　**b.** 可動の　　**c.** 検査　　**d.** 再課金する　　**e.** 最小の
**f.** 接続する・（電話で）つなぐ　　**g.** 態度　　**h.** 添付　　**i.** 内線・延長　　**j.** 保証（する）
**k.** 本文・文字データ・文字データを送る　　**l.** 毎月の　　**m.** 迷惑メール　　**n.** 郵便料金
**o.** 予約

## ■ Word Pairs  *Fill in each blank to complete the sentences.*

1. Could you (　　　　) me (　　　　) to Patrick Stewart?

2. While we were talking on the phone, he got angry and (　　　　)(　　　　).

3. I'm afraid you have the (　　　　)(　　　　).

4. I called the beauty salon to (　　　　) an (　　　　) for a haircut.

5. I gave the operator his (　　　　)(　　　　) and she transferred my call to him.

| | | |
|---|---|---|
| **a.** extension / number | **b.** put / through | **c.** hung / up |
| **d.** make / appointment | **e.** wrong / number | |

# Listening

## Listening Skill：英語の話の展開の特徴を知ろう

日本語では、話の結論を最後に述べることが多いのですが、英語には、大事なことや結論を先に述べ、理由や説明はその後に述べるという特徴があります。そのような特徴をふまえてリスニングをおこなうと、理解しやすくなります。

## Example 2-26

*You'll hear one conversation between two people and choose the best answer to the following question.*

**Woman**: Dr. Smith's office. May I help you?
**Man**: This is John Cohen. I'd like to (　　　) my appointment for an annual (　　　) on June 20th because I have to go on a (　　　) trip that day.
**Woman**: OK. Would you like to make an appointment on another day?
**Man**: Yes, but I'm not sure about my schedule now. I'll call you later.

**Question**: Why is John Cohen calling?
(A) He wants to make an appointment with his client.
(B) He wants to make an appointment for a safety check on his car.
(C) He wants to cancel an appointment for a haircut.
(D) He wants to cancel an appointment for a health checkup.

Ⓐ Ⓑ Ⓒ Ⓓ

## Part 1 Photographs

*You'll see a picture and hear four short statements. Choose the statement that best describes what you see in the picture.*

**1**

Ⓐ Ⓑ Ⓒ Ⓓ

**2** 2-28

Ⓐ Ⓑ Ⓒ Ⓓ

# Part 2 Question - Response  ((○))2-29,30,31,32

*You'll hear a question followed by three responses. Choose the best response to each question.*

3. Mark your answer on your answer sheet.  Ⓐ Ⓑ Ⓒ

4. Mark your answer on your answer sheet.  Ⓐ Ⓑ Ⓒ

5. Mark your answer on your answer sheet.  Ⓐ Ⓑ Ⓒ

6. Mark your answer on your answer sheet.  Ⓐ Ⓑ Ⓒ

# Part 3 Conversation  ((○))2-33,34

*You'll hear one conversation between two people and read three questions followed by four answers. Choose the best answer to each question.*

7. For how long does Solar Solutions guarantee its heating system?
   (A) Six months
   (B) One year
   (C) Three years
   (D) Five years

   Ⓐ Ⓑ Ⓒ Ⓓ

8. When will a service representative visit the woman's house?
   (A) Today
   (B) Tomorrow
   (C) The day after tomorrow
   (D) Next week

   Ⓐ Ⓑ Ⓒ Ⓓ

9. Which of the following words best describes the man's attitude?
   (A) Rude
   (B) Polite
   (C) Curious
   (D) Lazy

   Ⓐ Ⓑ Ⓒ Ⓓ

# Part 4 Talk 2-35,36

*You'll hear one talk and read three questions about the talk. The questions will be followed by four answers. Choose the best answer to each question.*

10. When is the restaurant closed?
   (A) Monday
   (B) Tuesday
   (C) Wednesday
   (D) Thursday

   Ⓐ Ⓑ Ⓒ Ⓓ

11. What time does the restaurant close in the evenings?
   (A)  9:00
   (B)  9:30
   (C) 10:00
   (D) 10:30

   Ⓐ Ⓑ Ⓒ Ⓓ

12. What was NOT mentioned as a feature of the restaurant?
   (A) There is a place to park your car.
   (B) You should reserve a table before going to the restaurant.
   (C) The restaurant has a special menu on Wednesdays.
   (D) The restaurant has a website.

   Ⓐ Ⓑ Ⓒ Ⓓ

---

## TOEIC 攻略のコツ：[新形式] Parts 6　文挿入問題の対策

Part 6の長文穴埋め問題では1つの本文につき設問は4問で、うち3問が語句挿入、1問が sentence挿入問題です。語句挿入問題では、下線が引かれている前後の1文を読めば解ける場合がほとんどですが、文挿入問題では、全体の文脈を理解する必要があるので、skimming をしてから解答しましょう。

# Reading

## 文法問題攻略のポイント：助動詞

1. can, could：能力「～できる」、許可「～してもよい」、可能性「～がありえる」など
   - 例1：My teacher **can** speak five languages.
   - 例2：**Can** I leave a message?
   - 例3：It **can** happen anywhere.
2. may：許可「～してもよい」、推量「～かもしれない」など
   - 例1：**May** I have your email address?
   - 例2：The client **may** visit us this afternoon.
3. must, have [has] to：義務「～しなければならない」、推量「～にちがいない」、否定 must not は禁止「～してはいけない」、don't [doesn't] have to は不必要「～しなくてもよい」など
   - 例1：I **must** make an appointment with the dentist right away.
   - 例2：You **must** be tired after finishing all these tasks.
4. should, ought to：義務「～すべきだ」、推量「～のはずだ」など
   - 例1：You **should** [**ought to**] tell the police what happened.
   - 例2：Our guests **should** [**ought to**] be home by now.
5. will, would：意志「～するつもりだ」、習性「よく～する[した]」、推量「～だろう」など
   - 例1：**I'll** be there in ten minutes.
   - 例2：She **would** call her mother every night.
   - 例3：It**'ll** be a sunny and warm day tomorrow.

## Part 5 Incomplete Sentences

*A word or phrase is missing in each sentence. Choose the best answer to complete the sentence.*

13. You ____ his phone number when he called.
    - (A) should ask
    - (B) would ask
    - (C) should have asked
    - (D) would have asked
    
    Ⓐ Ⓑ Ⓒ Ⓓ

14. If you receive an e-mail message with an attachment from someone you don't know, you ____ open it.
    - (A) ought
    - (B) ought to
    - (C) ought not to
    - (D) ought to have
    
    Ⓐ Ⓑ Ⓒ Ⓓ

15. I ____ rather call him now than be waiting for his call.
    - (A) would
    - (B) could
    - (C) should
    - (D) will
    
    Ⓐ Ⓑ Ⓒ Ⓓ

16. She is not answering her cell phone. She ____ it at home again.
    - (A) must leave
    - (B) has to leave
    - (C) must have left
    - (D) had to leave
    
    Ⓐ Ⓑ Ⓒ Ⓓ

# Part 6 Text Completion

*Read the following text. A word, phrase, or sentence is missing. Choose the best answer to complete the text.*

*Questions 17-19 refer to the following article.*

## Handwritten Letters

E-mail may have changed the way we communicate, but (    17    ). We are charmed by handwritten letters because they are rarer. People spend their time (    18    ) the paper, the envelope, and sometimes postage stamps. We pay more attention to handwritten letters than e-mail. Moreover, what spam (    19    ) come with a postage stamp on it?

17. (A) e-mail has a lot of security problems
    (B) we don't need the handwritten letter any more
    (C) we cannot live without e-mails
    (D) that doesn't mean the handwritten letter is dead

    Ⓐ Ⓑ Ⓒ Ⓓ

18. (A) choose
    (B) chose
    (C) choosing
    (D) chosen

    Ⓐ Ⓑ Ⓒ Ⓓ

19. (A) could
    (B) ought
    (C) must
    (D) had to

    Ⓐ Ⓑ Ⓒ Ⓓ

# Part 7 Reading Comprehension (Single Passages)

*Read the following texts. Each text or set of texts is followed by several questions. Choose the best answer to each question.*

*Questions 20-21 refer to the following article.*

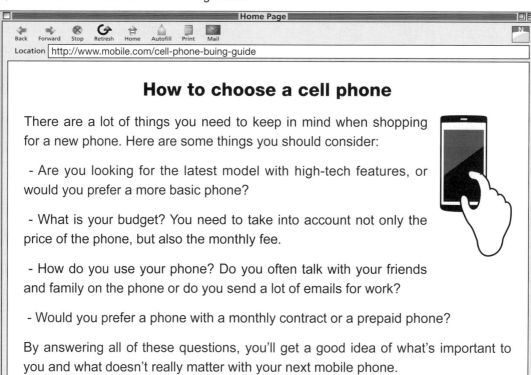

20. What is the article about?
   (A) Where to buy a phone
   (B) How to pick a phone
   (C) How to choose a carrier
   (D) How to use a phone

21. According to the article, what should you consider when you buy a new phone?
   (A) What functions you will need
   (B) What kind of design you would prefer
   (C) How long you will use the phone
   (D) What manufacturer made the phone

*Questions 22-24 refer to the following web advertisement.*

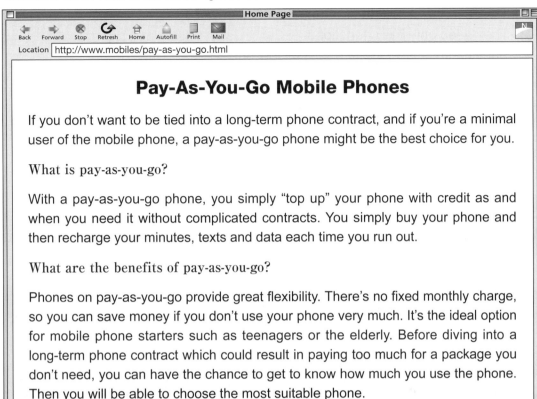

22. What is true about pay-as-you-go phones?
 (A) You pay by cash each time you make a call or send a text.
 (B) You pay a fixed monthly charge.
 (C) You buy a phone and recharge it when you need to.
 (D) After you buy a phone, you don't have to pay any call charges.

Ⓐ Ⓑ Ⓒ Ⓓ

23. What is an advantage of a pay-as-you-go phone?
 (A) Your phone calls are not charged at all.
 (B) You can save money if you are a minimal user.
 (C) You can get your phone for free.
 (D) You can use the phone anywhere in the world.

Ⓐ Ⓑ Ⓒ Ⓓ

**24.** Why is a pay-as-you-go phone a good choice for mobile phone starters?
  (A) They cannot choose their phone by themselves.
  (B) They need only basic functions.
  (C) They can buy a phone at a special low price.
  (D) They may not know how much they will use their phones.

Ⓐ Ⓑ Ⓒ Ⓓ

# Expand your vocabulary! —略語の本来の形を知ろう！

➤ **AI** : artificial intelligence「人工知能」
➤ **CEO** : Chief Executive Officer「最高経営責任者」
➤ **CV** : curriculum vitae「履歴書」
➤ **IT** : information technology「情報（通信）技術」
➤ **M&A** : mergers and acquisitions「（企業の）合併と吸収」
➤ **NGO** : nongovernmental organization「非政府組織」
➤ **NPO** : nonprofit organization「非営利組織」
➤ **PR** : public relations「広報活動」
➤ **UN** : the United Nations「国際連合」

# Learn more! — Vocabulary in Context

*Complete each English sentence according to its Japanese translation. The first letter is given.*

**1.** The operator said, "(H          )(o          ), please," so I held the line for fifteen minutes.
（交換手が「そのままお待ちください」と言ったので、私は15分間電話を切らなかった。）

**2.** She lives in the same city, so we can talk at (l          )(c          ) rates.
（彼女は同じ市内に住んでいるので、市内通話料金で話すことができる。）

**3.** As my daughter was living in another state, I spent a lot on (l          )
(d          ) calls every month.
（娘は他州に住んでいたので、長距離通話料金に毎月多額のお金がかかった。）

**4.** He (l          )(o          ) the telephone bill and put it in the drawer.
（彼は電話料金の請求書にざっと目を通すと、それを引き出しにしまった。）

---

1. Hold, on  2. local, call  3. long distance  4. looked over

# Unit 12
## Banking & Finance

このユニットでは、投資や貯金などの銀行業務と納税・請求書作成などの財務、それに予算作成を扱います。オフィスでお金がどう動いているかについて考えてみましょう。

## ■ Vocabulary   *Match each English word with its meaning in Japanese.* (CD)2-37

| | | |
|---|---|---|
| 1. balance ( ) | 2. budget ( ) | 3. currency ( ) |
| 4. deposit ( ) | 5. donate ( ) | 6. finance ( ) |
| 7. invest ( ) | 8. pension ( ) | 9. recession ( ) |
| 10. reduce ( ) | 11. teller ( ) | 12. transaction ( ) |
| 13. transfer ( ) | 14. vulnerable ( ) | 15. withdraw ( ) |

a. 移転・移す・送金する　　b. 寄付する　　c. 攻撃されやすい　　d. 財政・金融・融資する

e. 残高・均衡　　f. 通貨　　g. 投資する　　h. 取引　　i. 年金　　j. 引き出す・撤回する

k. 不景気　　l. 減らす　　m.（銀行の）窓口係　　n. 預金（する）　　o. 予算

## ■ Word Pairs   *Fill in each blank to complete the sentences.*

1. (　　　　　)(　　　　　) are going up these days.

2. At his death, my grandfather (　　　　) life (　　　　) amounting to $100,000.

3. Which would you like to open, a (　　　　)(　　　　) or a checking account?

4. Have you got any benefit from your (　　　　)(　　　　)?

5. Looking through the (　　　　)(　　　　), our manager expressed satisfaction with the outcome.

| | | |
|---|---|---|
| a. financial / report | b. stock / investment | c. savings / account |
| d. carried / insurance | e. bond / prices | |

# Listening

## Listening Skill：すべての語句を聞きとろうとしない

英語のリスニングでは、すべての語句を聞きとろうとするあまり、話の全体の流れが理解できなかったり、聞き逃したことで慌てたりすることがあります。しかし、すべての語句が聞きとれなくても、大体の意味はわかります。また、あらかじめ、何の情報が必要かわかっている場合は、その情報のみを聞きとるように注意を向けましょう。

### Example 2-38

*You'll hear one talk. Fill in the blanks and choose the best answer to the following question.*

We should inform you that if you keep at least $ (　　　　) on deposit in your checking account, there will be (　　　　)(　　　　) for writing checks. Otherwise, there will be a monthly charge. If you write very few checks each month, you may choose to pay a fee of (　　　　) cents per check.

**Question**: What would be required if you do not keep a regular balance in your checking account?

(A) 1,000 dollars a month
(B) 25 percent per check
(C) 25 cents per check
(D) No charge

Ⓐ Ⓑ Ⓒ Ⓓ

## Part 1 Photographs

*You'll see a picture and hear four short statements. Choose the statement that best describes what you see in the picture.*

**1**

Ⓐ Ⓑ Ⓒ Ⓓ

**2**

Ⓐ Ⓑ Ⓒ Ⓓ

106

# Part 2 Question - Response (CD) 2-41,42,43,44

*You'll hear a question followed by three responses. Choose the best response to each question.*

3. Mark your answer on your answer sheet.  Ⓐ Ⓑ Ⓒ

4. Mark your answer on your answer sheet.  Ⓐ Ⓑ Ⓒ

5. Mark your answer on your answer sheet.  Ⓐ Ⓑ Ⓒ

6. Mark your answer on your answer sheet.  Ⓐ Ⓑ Ⓒ


# Part 3 Conversation (CD) 2-45,46

*You'll hear one conversation between two people and read three questions followed by four answers. Choose the best answer to each question.*

7. How much will they have to cut the budget for next year?
   (A) 5 percent
   (B) 8 percent
   (C) 12 percent
   (D) 20 percent

   Ⓐ Ⓑ Ⓒ Ⓓ

8. What is the man's suggestion for cutting the budget?
   (A) Reduce energy expenses
   (B) Spend less on travel
   (C) Spend less on business entertaining
   (D) Require more face-to-face meetings

   Ⓐ Ⓑ Ⓒ Ⓓ

9. What is the woman's opinion?
   (A) The company should cut back on business travel.
   (B) The company should only allow economy-class business travel.
   (C) Business class should be used for domestic travel.
   (D) Business class should be used for international travel.

   Ⓐ Ⓑ Ⓒ Ⓓ

# Part 4 Talk 2-47,48

*You'll hear one talk and read three questions about the talk. The questions will be followed by four answers. Choose the best answer to each question.*

**10.** Who most likely is the speaker?
(A) A bank teller
(B) An accountant
(C) A loan officer
(D) A bank president ⒶⒷⒸⒹ

**11.** Look at the table. Which problem is the speaker most concerned about?

Customer Satisfaction Survey Results

| Rank | Complaint |
|------|-----------|
| 1 | Hidden fees |
| 2 | Bad customer service |
| 3 | Errors in account statements |
| 4 | Difficulty in applying for loans |
| 5 | Difficulties for small businesses |

(A) Hidden fees
(B) Bad customer service
(C) Errors in account statements
(D) Difficulty in applying for loans ⒶⒷⒸⒹ

**12.** What does the speaker think is the solution to the problem of hidden fees?
(A) Better accounting procedures
(B) New training programs for employees
(C) Better communication with customers
(D) Better communication with business owners ⒶⒷⒸⒹ

---

## TOEIC 攻略のコツ：[新形式] Part 7
## Multiple Passages問題の解き方

Part 7では single passage と2つまたは3つの文章の間につながりのある multiple passages が出題されます。multiple passages では指示文に内容が示されますので（例： Questions 186-190 refer to the following **list**, **schedule**, and **e-mail**)、内容を把握するヒントにしましょう。triple passages では、人材募集広告→応募書類→採用・不採用通知、商品やサービスの宣伝→問い合わせ・注文→返事、依頼状→承諾書→礼状などが典型的なパターンです。skimming で3つの文章のそれぞれの最初と最後の paragraph に目を通してどんな内容かを確認し、次に scanning でどの文に解答のヒントがあるかを探しましょう。複数の文章に渡っての設問は解くのに時間がかかるので後回しにしてもいいでしょう。

# Reading

## 文法問題攻略のポイント：接続詞

1. 等位接続詞［and, but, or, so, for, etc.］：名詞節と名詞節など、同等な語句や節をつなぐ。
    例1：Internet banking is common both in the U.S. **and** in the U.K.
    例2：I bought some stocks of the company, **for** I got to know it's going to market new products soon.
2. 従位接続詞は2つに分類される。
    (1) 名詞節を伴うもの：that, if, whether など
        例1：I know **that** we can expect a very low interest rate if we just use a savings account.
        例2：We are wondering **if** your bank could offer us a 500,000-dollar loan.
    (2) 副詞節を伴うもの：when, if, whether, as, because, though, so...that など
        例1：**When** I went to the life insurance company, a consultant gave me a full explanation of the benefits.
        例2：**Even if** I can get just a low interest rate, I will deposit my money in a bank account.
        例3：My old-age pension is **so** small **that** I could never live on it with ease.

## Part 5 Incomplete Sentences

*A word or phrase is missing in each sentence. Choose the best answer to complete the sentence.*

13. _____ I keep $1,000 in my bank account, does it pay any interest?
    (A) Unless      (C) Even if
    (B) If          (D) Even though

14. Your new checks will be mailed to you _____ they are ready.
    (A) as far as   (C) as soon as
    (B) as long as  (D) as late as

15. I again propose _____ we go ahead with this new investment even though there is still some risk.
    (A) if          (C) what
    (B) that        (D) so

16. Credit is valuable. That is _____ you need to know what you should do if you have credit problems.
    (A) because     (C) how
    (B) why         (D) where

# Part 6 Text Completion

*Read the following text. A word, phrase, or sentence is missing. Choose the best answer to complete the text.*

*Questions 17-19 refer to the following advertisement.*

## Don't Miss the Hottest e-Finance Technology Event in 20XX!

Online transactions are at the heart of business today ( **17** ) they are part of the integrated e-Finance applications that run a company, or the e-Finance transactions that drive new revenue. With rapid increases in the amount of money spent on online goods and services, ( **18** ). Survival in today's business world requires ( **19** ) companies not just understand new technology, but actively accept the changes.

The TechnoBIT Toronto 20XX Finance Exposition will showcase present solutions that will enable your business to set up an effective e-Finance platform and provide the tools required for efficiently managing and reporting on this rapidly growing channel.

17. (A) whether      (B) if      (C) though      (D) so

    Ⓐ Ⓑ Ⓒ Ⓓ

18. (A) manufacturers are required to develop new products
    (B) the changes to e-Finance technology cannot be ignored
    (C) the government needs to make new regulations
    (D) consumers want to save their money

    Ⓐ Ⓑ Ⓒ Ⓓ

19. (A) what      (B) whether      (C) that      (D) if

    Ⓐ Ⓑ Ⓒ Ⓓ

# Part 7 Reading Comprehension (Triple Passages)

*Read the following texts. Each text or set of texts is followed by several questions. Choose the best answer to each question.*

*Questions 20-24 refer to the following advertisement and e-mails.*

## On-line Banking Organization (OBO)

Online Banking Organization (OBO) can help you manage savings and checking accounts, apply for loans, or pay bills quickly and easily. Online banking, a service provided by many banks, allows you to conduct banking transactions using a personal computer and mobile telephone. You can:

- Access accounts round-the-clock, even on weekends
- Transfer funds between accounts
- Download information directly into personal finance software
- Receive and pay bills on-line

If you choose an "Internet-only" bank, you may no longer have access to a local branch. Some Internet-only banks, however, offer higher interest rates and lower fees than traditional banks. If you decide to shop for a bank on the Internet, check to see that the Online Banking Organization insures your bank's deposits.

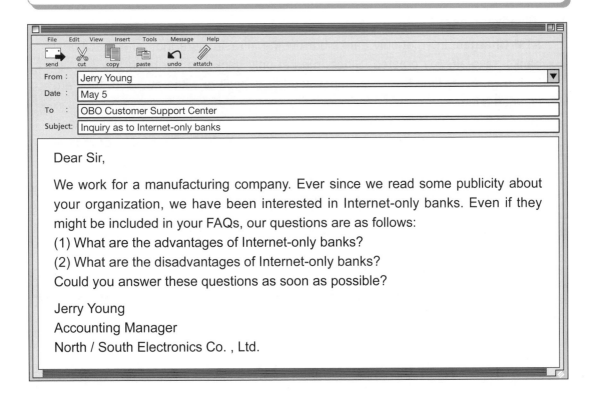

From: Jerry Young
Date: May 5
To: OBO Customer Support Center
Subject: Inquiry as to Internet-only banks

Dear Sir,

We work for a manufacturing company. Ever since we read some publicity about your organization, we have been interested in Internet-only banks. Even if they might be included in your FAQs, our questions are as follows:
(1) What are the advantages of Internet-only banks?
(2) What are the disadvantages of Internet-only banks?
Could you answer these questions as soon as possible?

Jerry Young
Accounting Manager
North / South Electronics Co., Ltd.

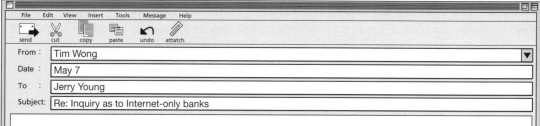

Dear Mr. Jerry Young,

Thank you for your inquiry.
Here are some advantages and disadvantages of Internet-only banks.

### Advantages

**Lower Fees**: As Internet-only banks exist in the virtual world, they don't need human staff or expensive locations. This obviously saves them a lot of money and it enables them to offer services to customers much more cheaply than traditional banks.

**Higher Interest**: The cost savings also result in these banks offering higher interest rates to their customers. This is the reason why many customers prefer to keep their funds with these banks, instead of banks that have much longer legacies.

**Services**: Internet-only banks allow your data to be transferred to a personal finance app for analysis. The app provides you budgeting tips and forecasts your finances.

### Disadvantages

**ATM Charges**: Internet-only banks borrow the infrastructure that other traditional banks have already created. Since Internet-only banks do not have any ATM of their own, every time their customers need to deposit or withdraw cash, they are charged a fee.

**Lack of human contact**: Banks usually develop a deep relationship with their client. A certain amount of human contact is required to build a relationship of mutual trust. This is where online banks cannot compete with traditional banks.

**Security**: It is not uncommon for hackers to access bank details of other people. Internet-only banks are vulnerable to such attacks.

Tim Wong
Unit Chief
OBO Customer Support Center

**20.** What is On-line Banking Organization?
 (A) A group which advertises traditional banks
 (B) A group which helps people deposit or withdraw money over the Internet
 (C) A group which helps people open up a traditional bank account through the Internet
 (D) A group which provides people with some information about computers

Ⓐ Ⓑ Ⓒ Ⓓ

**21.** Why is it possible for Internet-only banks to offer higher interest rates and lower fees than traditional banks?
 (A) They have more floating capital than traditional banks.
 (B) Their operational costs are lower than that of traditional banks.
 (C) They make money in online advertising.
 (D) They work as agents for traditional banks.

Ⓐ Ⓑ Ⓒ Ⓓ

**22.** Which department is Jerry Young most probably in?
 (A) The sales department
 (B) The personnel department
 (C) The planning department
 (D) The financial department

Ⓐ Ⓑ Ⓒ Ⓓ

**23.** Why do Internet-only bank customers have to pay ATM charges?
 (A) Internet-only banks have only a limited number of ATMs.
 (B) Internet-only bank customers have to use ATMs owned by other banks.
 (C) Internet-only banks have to make money from ATM charges.
 (D) Internet-only banks do not have a depositing function.

Ⓐ Ⓑ Ⓒ Ⓓ

**24.** Which of the following is true about Internet-only banks?
 (A) Security is strong enough to prevent any hackers' attack.
 (B) Customers are likely to build a deep relationship with banks.
 (C) Customers can get financial suggestions through the personal software.
 (D) Customers can access their accounts on weekdays but not on weekends.

Ⓐ Ⓑ Ⓒ Ⓓ

# **E**xpand your vocabulary! —語源をつきとめよう！

➤ **legere** 「読む・集める」[ラテン語] → legend, lecture, lesson, collect, neglect, select
➤ **manus** 「手」[ラテン語] → manner, manufacture, manuscript, manual, manage
➤ **men** 「考える」[印欧祖語] → mind, mention
➤ **mensis** 「測る」[印欧祖語] → moon, meal, measure, meter
➤ **pendere** 「ぶら下がる」[ラテン語] → pendant, depend, suspend, expend, independence
➤ **populus** 「民衆」[ラテン語] → people, popular, public, publish, publicity
➤ **portus** 「(陸の)入り口」[ラテン語] → port, passport, import, export, transport
➤ **pressura** 「苦痛・苦難・圧力」[ラテン語] → press, pressure, impress, express, depress, suppress

# **L**earn more! — **V**ocabulary in **C**ontext

*Complete each English sentence according to its Japanese translation. The first letter is given.*

1. As regards our financial standing, please (r        )(t        ) CLD Bank, San Francisco Branch.
(当社の財務状況につきましては、CLD 銀行サンフランシスコ支店にご照会下さい。)

2. The firm you inquired about is a highly reliable and well-established organization, which (e        ) a good (r        ) in this city.
(お問い合わせの会社は非常に信頼の置ける老舗で、当市では高い評判を受けております。)

3. If you have not subscribed to this journal, (m        )(s        ) to do so.
(まだ本ジャーナルを購読していないなら、必ず購読してください。)

4. We are keen to get involved in (f        )(i        ).
(我が社は財政統合に非常に興味があります。)

---

1. refer to  2. enjoys, reputation  3. make, sure  4. financial integration

# Unit 13
## Office Work & Equipment

このユニットでは、会社の一般的な業務と事務機器・用品などのトピックを取り扱います。
オフィスでの仕事の進め方や、どんな事務機器が使われているのかを理解しましょう。

■ **Vocabulary** *Match each English word with its meaning in Japanese.* 🎧2-49

| | | |
|---|---|---|
| 1. achieve ( ) | 2. comfort ( ) | 3. conference ( ) |
| 4. document ( ) | 5. encourage ( ) | 6. internal ( ) |
| 7. maintain ( ) | 8. proposal ( ) | 9. reject ( ) |
| 10. replace ( ) | 11. revise ( ) | 12. second-hand ( ) |
| 13. surplus ( ) | 14. thermal ( ) | 15. undergo ( ) |

**a.** 余り　　**b.** 維持する　　**c.** 受ける　　**d.** 会議　　**e.** 快適さ　　**f.** 拒絶する

**g.** 修正する　　**h.** 奨励する　　**i.** 書類　　**j.** 達成する　　**k.** 中古の

**l.** 提案　　**m.** 取り替える　　**n.** 内部の　　**o.** 熱の・温度の

■ **Word Pairs** *Fill in each blank to complete the sentences.*

1. We need to (　　　　　) our (　　　　　) to make it better.

2. The new manager will be (　　　　)(　　　　　) of the project.

3. Every section of the company has to (　　　　　) an internal (　　　　　) once a year.

4. Our products need to (　　　　　) the international (　　　　　).

5. To his disappointment, the manager did not (　　　　　)(　　　　　) his work.

| | | |
|---|---|---|
| **a.** meet / standards | **b.** revise / plan | **c.** approve / of |
| **d.** undergo / inspection | **e.** in / charge | |

115

# Listening

## Listening Skill：繰り返し出てくる語句に注意しよう

ある会話や発話の中で繰り返し出てくる語句や関連する語句は、トピックや話の流れを理解するための重要な手掛かりです。意識して聞きましょう。

## Example 2-50

*You'll hear one talk. Fill in the blanks and choose the best answer to the following question.*

At HLS (        )(         ), you'll always find the greatest goods at whatever prices you can afford. We offer a lot of (         )(         ) ranging from (         ) to (         ). We have whatever you need throughout the year. Please visit our store and find what you have been looking for.

**Question:** What can you NOT buy at this store?
 (A) Computers
 (B) Printers
 (C) Copying machines
 (D) Washing machines

　　　　　　　　　　　　Ⓐ Ⓑ Ⓒ Ⓓ

## Part 1 Photographs

*You'll see a picture and hear four short statements. Choose the statement that best describes what you see in the picture.*

**1**

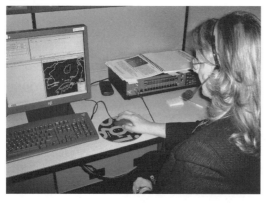

　　　　　　Ⓐ Ⓑ Ⓒ Ⓓ

**2**

　　　　　　Ⓐ Ⓑ Ⓒ Ⓓ

# Part 2 Question - Response ((CD))2-53,54,55,56

*You'll hear a question followed by three responses. Choose the best response to each question.*

3. Mark your answer on your answer sheet. Ⓐ Ⓑ Ⓒ

4. Mark your answer on your answer sheet. Ⓐ Ⓑ Ⓒ

5. Mark your answer on your answer sheet. Ⓐ Ⓑ Ⓒ

6. Mark your answer on your answer sheet. Ⓐ Ⓑ Ⓒ


# Part 3 Short Conversation ((CD))2-57,58

*You'll hear one conversation with three people and read three questions followed by four answers. Choose the best answer to each question.*

7. Why do they want to buy new office furniture and equipment now?
   (A) They are moving to a new office.
   (B) They have a budget surplus this year.
   (C) They will not be able to afford new furniture in next year's budget.
   (D) The furniture they have now is old.

   Ⓐ Ⓑ Ⓒ Ⓓ

8. What does the woman hope will happen next year?
   (A) The company will move to a new location.
   (B) They will be able to afford to buy new filing cabinets.
   (C) There will be money available to buy office equipment.
   (D) The company will develop a new ten-year plan.

   Ⓐ Ⓑ Ⓒ Ⓓ

9. What are they going to buy this year?
   (A) Second-hand desks
   (B) New desks
   (C) Second-hand filing cabinets
   (D) New filing cabinets

   Ⓐ Ⓑ Ⓒ Ⓓ

# Part 4 Talk 🎧 2-59,60

*You'll hear one talk and read three questions about the talk. The questions will be followed by four answers. Choose the best answer to each question.*

**10.** Where would you hear this?
 (A) In a TV commercial
 (B) At a business meeting
 (C) In a TV business news report
 (D) In a business consultant's speech

Ⓐ Ⓑ Ⓒ Ⓓ

**11.** Which of the following products are most likely for sale at Office Express?
 (A) Filing cabinets
 (B) Computers
 (C) Microwave ovens
 (D) Televisions

Ⓐ Ⓑ Ⓒ Ⓓ

**12.** Which of the following does Office Express offer to its customers?
 (A) Free shipping on all products
 (B) A 30-day guarantee on all products
 (C) A 90-day guarantee on all products
 (D) A 120-day guarantee on some products

Ⓐ Ⓑ Ⓒ Ⓓ

---

### TOEIC 攻略のコツ：［新形式］Part 7　文挿入問題の対策

Part 7読解問題での文挿入問題は、長文中に［1］〜［4］の空所があり、設問に "In which of the positions marked [1], [2], [3], and [4] does the following sentence best belong?" とその後に空所に入る sentence が与えられているものです。その sentence の意味を正確に把握することはもちろんですが、全体の文脈をつかむことが重要なので、skimming をしましょう。この問題は時間がかかることが多いので最後に解きましょう。

# Reading

## 文法問題攻略のポイント：関係代名詞＆関係副詞

1. 関係代名詞：先行詞が人の場合には who（主格・《略式》目的格）、whom（目的格）を用い、物の場合には which（主格・目的格）を用いる。目的格の関係代名詞は省略できる。that は人・物、主格・目的格のいずれにも使用できる。所有格の whose は人・物のどちらにも使用できる。
   例1：I know that woman **who** [**that**] is making copies now.
   例2：Can you see the building **whose** roof is blue? Our company is there.
   which は前の文またはその一部を先行詞とすることもある。
   例：I was late for a meeting yesterday, **which** made my boss very angry.
2. 関係副詞：where の先行詞は場所・状況・立場、when は時、why は理由、how は方法である。（how の場合、先行詞 the way と一緒に用いない。）
   例：Our proposal was very attractive. I don't know the reason **why** it was rejected.
3. 先行詞だけでは、関係代名詞と関係副詞のどちらを選択するかは判断できない。後ろの文中で主格・所有格・目的格になっている場合は関係代名詞、副詞として働いている場合は関係副詞が用いられる。
   例：This is the reason **which** my boss gave us when he introduced a new computer system.

## Part 5  Incomplete Sentences

*A word or phrase is missing in each sentence. Choose the best answer to complete the sentence.*

13. This is the warehouse _____ I used to visit in my rookie year at the company.
    (A) which          (C) where
    (B) when           (D) in which

14. This is a case _____ we should be careful when we start a new project.
    (A) what           (C) which
    (B) why            (D) where

15. You should complete the documents by Friday, _____ we are supposed to submit them to the local government.
    (A) which          (C) when
    (B) where          (D) why

16. Please deliver this document to AIC Company, _____ office is located in Chicago.
    (A) which          (C) where
    (B) whose          (D) that

119

# Part 6 Text Completion

*Read the following text. A word, phrase, or sentence is missing. Choose the best answer to complete the text.*

Questions 17-19 refer to the following e-mail.

To all staff:

The company is planning to create a new company logo. A company logo helps create a new image of the company. (    17    ). We encourage you to submit your original designs. If you are interested, please contact us. We will send you a guide (    18    ) shows all the ways you can submit your designs. Don't miss this opportunity (    19    ) you can show your creativity.

Walter Robbins
P. R. Director

17. (A) Create a logo for your company with our free online logo maker.
    (B) We have chosen the best logo design on the basis of a competition.
    (C) We are proud of the long history of our company logo.
    (D) That is the reason why we have decided to change our logo.

18. (A) why    (B) how    (C) where    (D) which

19. (A) why    (B) how    (C) where    (D) which

# Part 7 Reading Comprehension

*Read the following texts. Each text or set of texts is followed by several questions. Choose the best answer to each question.*

Questions 20-22 refer to the following article.

## Thermal Comfort

To have "thermal comfort" means that a person feels neither too cold nor too warm. —[1]— Therefore, maintaining constant thermal conditions in the office is important. It can be achieved only when the air temperature, humidity and air movement are within the exact range often referred to as the "comfort zone." —[2]— A general recommendation is that the temperature be held constant in the range of 21-23°C (69-73°F). In summertime, it is advisable to keep airconditioned offices slightly warmer to decrease the temperature difference between indoors and outdoors. —[3]— We recommend that relative humidity be maintained below 60 percent. There is no recommended lower level of humidity for achieving thermal comfort, but very low humidity can lead to health problems.—[4]— The relative humidity should be greater than 30 percent.

The next table shows the acceptable ranges of temperature.

| Conditions | Acceptable temperatures | |
|---|---|---|
| | °C | °F |
| **Summer** | | |
| Relative humidity 30% | 24.5-28 | 76-82 |
| Relative humidity 60% | 23-25.5 | 74-78 |
| **Winter** | | |
| Relative humidity 30% | 20.5-25.5 | 69-78 |
| Relative humidity 60% | 20-24 | 68-75 |

20. What is true about the conditions in the office?
   (A) You should often change the temperature.
   (B) You should keep the temperature lower when it is hot outdoors.
   (C) You should maintain the humidity between 30-60 percent.
   (D) The lower the humidity is, the better it may be.

Ⓐ Ⓑ Ⓒ Ⓓ

21. In which of the positions marked [1], [2], [3], and [4] does the following sentence best belong?

"Thermal comfort is important both for one's health and for productivity"

(A) [1]   (B) [2]   (C) [3]   (D) [4]

22. Which statement is true about the table?
(A) In summer, the temperature should be maintained lower than in winter.
(B) In summer, the temperature should be maintained higher than in winter.
(C) In winter, the temperature should be maintained higher than in summer.
(D) When the humidity is relatively low, the acceptable temperature is relatively low.

*Questions 23-24 refer to the following online chat discussion.*

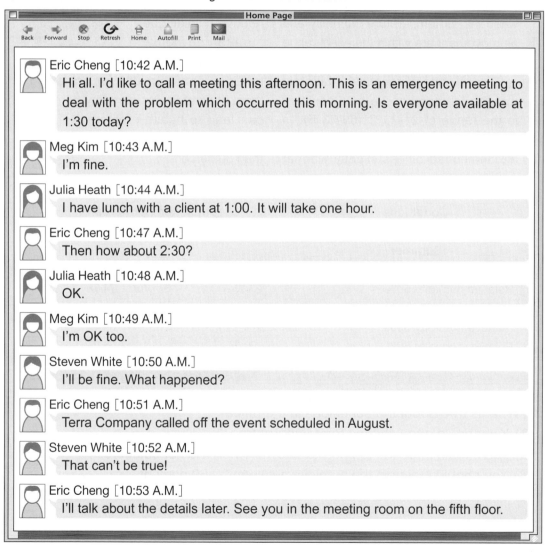

**23.** What time will the meeting start?
(A) 1 : 00 P.M.
(B) 1 : 30 P.M.
(C) 2 : 00 P.M.
(D) 2 : 30 P.M.                              Ⓐ Ⓑ Ⓒ Ⓓ

**24.** What is the problem?
(A) Their client didn't come to lunch.
(B) Their client canceled a meeting with them.
(C) An event was canceled.
(D) An order was canceled.                  Ⓐ Ⓑ Ⓒ Ⓓ

# Expand your vocabulary! —イディオムに強くなろう！(1)

➢ **account for**「～を説明する」
➢ **be concerned about**「～を心配する」
➢ **bound for**「～行きの」
➢ **figure out**「～を理解する」
➢ **get rid of**「～を取り除く」

➢ **in case**「～に備えて」
➢ **out of date**「時代遅れの」
➢ **run out of**「～を使い果たす」
➢ **take advantage of**「～を利用する」

# Learn more! — Vocabulary in Context

*Complete each English sentence according to its Japanese translation. The first letter is given.*

1. Documents including (p        )(i        ) should be classified as confidential.
   （個人情報を含む書類は、部外秘として分類されるべきである。）

2. (T      )(w      ) handle a lot of routine work.
   （臨時社員はたくさんの日常業務を処理している。）

3. We need to discuss and determine which (a      )(p      ) we should carry out.
   （われわれはどの代替案を実行すべきかを、話し合って決める必要がある。）

4. You must get permission (i      )(a      ) before using the conference room.
   （その会議室を使うには、事前に許可を得なければならない。）

---

1. personal information　2. Temporary workers　3. alternative plan　4. in advance

# Unit 14
## Housing & Properties

このユニットでは住宅や不動産を扱います。その内容は土地の取得、住宅の契約・設計・建設・引越しから公共料金の支払いにまでに及んでいます。

■ **Vocabulary** *Match each English word with its meaning in Japanese.* 2-61

1. condominium (　) 　　2. construction (　) 　　3. cottage (　)
4. countryside (　) 　　5. dormitory (　) 　　6. landlord (　)
7. neighborhood (　) 　　8. property (　) 　　9. quote (　)
10. real estate (　) 　　11. region (　) 　　12. rent (　)
13. rural (　) 　　14. sustainable (　) 　　15. urban (　)

a. 田舎［田園］の 　　b. 田舎・田園地方 　　c. 近所 　　d. 建設 　　e. 財産・特性
f. 耐久性がある・持続可能な 　　g. 地主・家主 　　h. 地方・地帯 　　i. 都会の
j. 不動産 　　k. 別荘・小住居 　　l. （分譲）マンション 　　m. 見積り額
n. 家賃・地代・賃貸（賃借）する 　　o. 寮

■ **Word Pairs** *Fill in each blank to complete the sentences.*

1. I went to see my landlord yesterday to (　　　　) the (　　　　).

2. The (　　　　)(　　　　) building is 40 stories high.

3. If you live in the center of the city, you can make use of (　　　　) (　　　　) systems like the subway.

4. We should seek (　　　　)(　　　　) instead of rapid economic growth.

5. You are required to (　　　　)(　　　　) in writing at least 30 days before leaving.

| a. newly / constructed | b. give / notice | c. renew / contract |
| d. sustainable / development | e. convenient / transportation | |

# Listening

## Listening Skill：頭の中で日本語に訳さない

頭の中でいちいち日本語に訳していたのでは、処理が間に合わなくなり、結局話の流れもわからなくなってしまいます。聞いた順番に、英語のまま意味を理解できるよう練習しましょう。

### Example 2-62

*You'll hear one talk. Fill in the blanks and choose the best answer to the following question.*

Hello. This is Tim Cooper, Kangaroo Moving Company agent. Thank you very much for your call. For a family of five, your (          )(          ) will be about $2,000 to $3,000, depending on the size of the house, location, number of bedrooms and so on. To Atlanta, it would take (          )(          ). A truck would be sent to your home in the morning and your (          ) would be set in place in your new home by the evening of that day.
To get a quote, please access our website. Thanks again.

**Question**: Look at the request form. What kind of residence does the customer live in now?

(A) Apartment with Elevator
(B) Apartment with Stairs
(C) House with Stairs
(D) House No Stairs

| Request a Moving Quote | |
|---|---|
| Moving from Zip | 30077 |
| The Location | Apartment with Stairs |
| Moving to Zip | 30313 |
| The Location | House No Stairs |

Ⓐ Ⓑ Ⓒ Ⓓ

## Part 1  Photographs

*You'll see a picture and hear four short statements. Choose the statement that best describes what you see in the picture.*

**1**

Ⓐ Ⓑ Ⓒ Ⓓ

**2**

Ⓐ Ⓑ Ⓒ Ⓓ

125

# Part 2 Question - Response  (CD) 2-65,66,67,68

You'll hear a question followed by three responses. Choose the best response to each question.

3. Mark your answer on your answer sheet.  Ⓐ Ⓑ Ⓒ

4. Mark your answer on your answer sheet.  Ⓐ Ⓑ Ⓒ

5. Mark your answer on your answer sheet.  Ⓐ Ⓑ Ⓒ

6. Mark your answer on your answer sheet.  Ⓐ Ⓑ Ⓒ


# Part 3 Conversation  (CD) 2-69,70

You'll hear one conversation between two people and read three questions followed by four answers. Choose the best answer to each question.

7. What is the man's job?
   (A) Travel agent
   (B) Taxi driver
   (C) Real estate agent
   (D) Traffic officer

   Ⓐ Ⓑ Ⓒ Ⓓ

8. Look at the map. Where is the subway station?

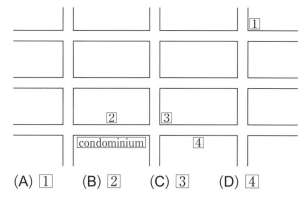

   (A) 1    (B) 2    (C) 3    (D) 4

   Ⓐ Ⓑ Ⓒ Ⓓ

9. When did the man suggest meeting?
   (A) Thirty minutes from now
   (B) Tomorrow afternoon
   (C) This morning
   (D) Tomorrow morning

   Ⓐ Ⓑ Ⓒ Ⓓ

# Part 4 Talk ((CD))2-71,72

*You'll hear one talk and read three questions about the talk. The questions will be followed by four answers. Choose the best answer to each question.*

10. What is the subject of this talk?
   (A) A news report on the housing industry
   (B) An advertisement for a vacation home construction company
   (C) A real estate agency advertisement
   (D) A job advertisement for fully licensed real estate agents

   (A)(B)(C)(D)

11. Where does this company conduct its business?
   (A) In the east region
   (B) In the west region
   (C) In the northeast region
   (D) In the northwest region

   (A)(B)(C)(D)

12. Who should call this company?
   (A) People who want to discuss their pension plans
   (B) People who want to talk to a travel agent
   (C) People who want to buy a house in an urban area
   (D) People who want to buy a house in a rural area

   (A)(B)(C)(D)

---

### TOEIC 攻略のコツ：[新形式] Part 7　表現の意図を問う設問対策

Part 7 では What does（人）mean when he/she writes "…"? という形式で、文書中の表現の意図を問う設問が出題されますが、その1文からだけでは意図が判断できないことがあります。例えば、We've enough potatoes の意図を問われている場合、「十分ポテトの在庫があるので買う必要がない」のか「食卓で十分ポテトを食べたのでもういらない」のか、わかりません。本文中のその文の前後をよく読んで判断するようにしましょう。

# ■ Reading

## 文法問題攻略のポイント：前置詞

1. 場所を表す前置詞（句）には注意が必要！
   - 例1：My house is located **in** the suburbs of Chicago.
   - 例2：He lives **at** 303 Club Quarters, Philadelphia.
   - 例3：We are looking for a condominium **on** this street.
2. 時を表す前置詞（句）にも気をつけよう！
   - 例1：I usually arrive at the office **at** 8:30 **in** the morning.
   - 例2：We moved to this house **on** the morning of October 12th.
3. まぎらわしい前置詞［until, till, by, before, etc.］には特に要注意！
   - 例1：I'm going to stay here **until**［**till**］tomorrow morning.
   - 例2：I must leave here **by** noon tomorrow.
4. 名詞句が副詞的に働き前置詞が用いられない場合がある。
   - 例1：I bought the chairs **last year**.
   - 例2：I walk the dog in the park **every morning**.
5. 前置詞を用いた慣用句はたくさんある。
   - 例：The building **in front of** my apartment house is **under construction**.

# Part 5 Incomplete Sentences

*A word or phrase is missing in each sentence. Choose the best answer to complete the sentence.*

13. The subway station is only a ten-minute walk ____ here.
- (A) in
- (B) from
- (C) of
- (D) out of

ⒶⒷⒸⒹ

14. I will pick you up _____ one hour to drive you to the apartment you want to check.
- (A) at
- (B) on
- (C) in
- (D) about

ⒶⒷⒸⒹ

15. You have a room here _____ two windows looking out on the little park.
- (A) of
- (B) at
- (C) in
- (D) with

ⒶⒷⒸⒹ

16. We should drop in at the real estate agency ____ our way home.
- (A) at
- (B) in
- (C) on
- (D) under

ⒶⒷⒸⒹ

# Part 6 Text Completion

*Read the following text. A word, phrase, or sentence is missing. Choose the best answer to complete the text.*

*Questions 17-19 refer to the following information.*

## Rental Contract

The contract is valid (    17    ) one year starting tomorrow, renewable. (    18    ). This is subject to change if you decide to renew (    19    ) the end of one year. There is a two-month deposit, which can be returned if there is no damage to the apartment.
Sign two copies of the contract.

17. (A) for
    (B) in
    (C) to
    (D) at

Ⓐ Ⓑ Ⓒ Ⓓ

18. (A) Rent is $2,000.
    (B) The housing loan carries 3.5 percent interest.
    (C) The apartment has two bedrooms.
    (D) Pets are allowed.

Ⓐ Ⓑ Ⓒ Ⓓ

19. (A) in
    (B) until
    (C) at
    (D) to

Ⓐ Ⓑ Ⓒ Ⓓ

# Part 7 Reading Comprehension

*Read the following texts. Each text or set of texts is followed by several questions. Choose the best answer to each question.*

Questions 20-24 refer to the following advertisement and an e-mail.

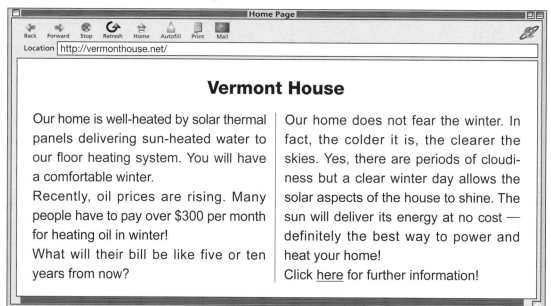

**Vermont House**

Our home is well-heated by solar thermal panels delivering sun-heated water to our floor heating system. You will have a comfortable winter.

Recently, oil prices are rising. Many people have to pay over $300 per month for heating oil in winter!

What will their bill be like five or ten years from now?

Our home does not fear the winter. In fact, the colder it is, the clearer the skies. Yes, there are periods of cloudiness but a clear winter day allows the solar aspects of the house to shine. The sun will deliver its energy at no cost — definitely the best way to power and heat your home!

Click here for further information!

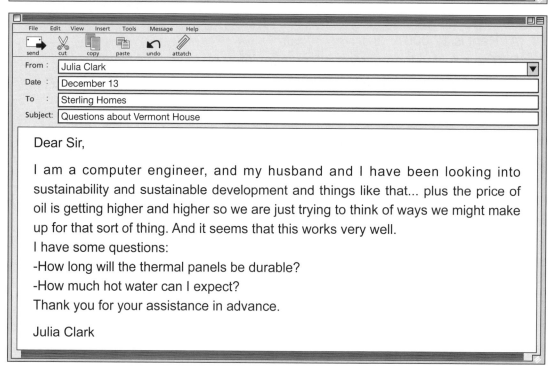

From: Julia Clark
Date: December 13
To: Sterling Homes
Subject: Questions about Vermont House

Dear Sir,

I am a computer engineer, and my husband and I have been looking into sustainability and sustainable development and things like that... plus the price of oil is getting higher and higher so we are just trying to think of ways we might make up for that sort of thing. And it seems that this works very well.

I have some questions:
-How long will the thermal panels be durable?
-How much hot water can I expect?
Thank you for your assistance in advance.

Julia Clark

20. Who is most likely to have written the first passage?
   (A) A person who wants to sell a house
   (B) A person who wants to sell solar panels
   (C) A person who wants to sell floor heating system
   (D) A person who wants to promote environmental protection

   Ⓐ Ⓑ Ⓒ Ⓓ

21. What is unique about the Vermont House?
   (A) It uses winter snow.
   (B) It uses solar energy.
   (C) It uses water power.
   (D) It uses cold temperature.

   Ⓐ Ⓑ Ⓒ Ⓓ

22. Why does Vermont House not fear winter?
   (A) Hot water melts snow.
   (B) The weather is more likely to be sunny in winter.
   (C) It produces more energy on cloudy days.
   (D) Solar panels produce power even when it snows.

   Ⓐ Ⓑ Ⓒ Ⓓ

23. Why is Julia interested in Vermont House?
   (A) She doesn't have to use the floor heating system.
   (B) She can live with her husband.
   (C) She doesn't have to pay much for oil.
   (D) She can see beautiful scenery.

   Ⓐ Ⓑ Ⓒ Ⓓ

24. What is Julia concerned about?
   (A) How much it will cost to install thermal panels
   (B) How much oil bills will be
   (C) How long thermal panels will last
   (D) What maintenance is required

   Ⓐ Ⓑ Ⓒ Ⓓ

## **E**xpand your vocabulary! —イディオムに強くなろう！(2)

- **agree with** [**to**]「～に同意する」
- **apologize for**「～をわびる」
- **be familiar with**「～をよく知っている」
- **benefit from**「～から恩恵を受ける」
- **comply with**「～に従う」

- **in charge of**「～の責任を負って」
- **nothing but**「～しかない」
- **pull～ over**「～を道に止めさせる」
- **put～ away**「～を片付ける」

## **L**earn more! — **V**ocabulary in **C**ontext

*Complete each English sentence according to its Japanese translation. The first letter is given.*

1. The rooms are luxuriously furnished and the kitchen is (f          )(e        ).
（部屋には豪華な家具が備えられ、台所には設備が完全に整っています。）

2. The house (r       ) is $2,500, including all (u       ).
（家賃は電気・水道・ガス、一切込みで2500ドルです。）

3. I could help you (m       ) in and tell you about the (n       ).
（お引越しのお手伝いと、ご近所についてご説明できるでしょう。）

4. My (l      )(t      ) boasts a clean and healthy (e       ).
（私の地元の町はきれいで健康に良い環境を誇っています。）

---

1. fully, equipped　2. rent, utilities　3. move, neighborhood　4. local, town, environment

# Unit 15

## Business & Management

このユニットでは、ビジネス業務と経営を扱います。ビジネス会議・顧客との交渉・秘書とのやりとり・マーケティングなどがトピックになります。

### ■ Vocabulary  *Match each English word with its meaning in Japanese.*  CD 2-73

| | | |
|---|---|---|
| 1. acquire ( ) | 2. agenda ( ) | 3. cooperate ( ) |
| 4. deserve ( ) | 5. dismiss ( ) | 6. goal ( ) |
| 7. invoice ( ) | 8. negotiate ( ) | 9. prediction ( ) |
| 10. publish ( ) | 11. pursue ( ) | 12. revenue ( ) |
| 13. settle ( ) | 14. shareholder ( ) | 15. suggestion ( ) |

**a.** （〜に）値する　　**b.** 追い求める　　**c.** 送り状・請求書　　**d.** 解雇する　　**e.** 獲得する

**f.** 株主　　**g.** 議題　　**h.** 協力する　　**i.** 交渉する　　**j.** 収入・歳入

**k.** 出版する　　**l.** 提案　　**m.** 定住させる・解決する　　**n.** 目標　　**o.** 予測

### ■ Word Pairs  *Fill in each blank to complete the sentences.*

1. We do not just (　　　　)(　　　　　) but promote social welfare.

2. It is (　　　　)(　　　　　) to hold our market shares together.

3. Our products have a (　　　　)(　　　　　) of 35 percent in the U.S.

4. Most employees were very tired because they had to (　　　　)(　　　　　).

5. We are going to (　　　　)(　　　　　) the manufacturer for a discount.

| | | |
|---|---|---|
| **a.** market / share | **b.** pursue / profits | **c.** mutually / convenient |
| **d.** negotiate / with | **e.** work / overtime | |

# Listening

## Listening Skill：最後まで集中力を持続させよう

聞きとれない箇所があったり、わかない単語があったりしても、最後まで聞いているうちに、話が理解できることもあります。あきらめないで、最後まで集中力を持続させましょう。

### Example 2-74

*You'll hear one talk. Fill in the blanks and choose the best answer to the following question.*

Thanks, Jane and all of you. Jane, your comments about my (　　　　) are much more than it really deserves. I have so many other people to thank, my good friends, my family, the staff of AIM (　　　　) and all those who helped me (　　　　) the (　　　　). Without their help and support, my efforts would not have led to this success today. This award is really for them. Thank you once again.

**Question**: Who is this person?
 (A) A writer's agent
 (B) A writer
 (C) A publisher
 (D) The chairperson of the meeting

　　　　　　　Ⓐ Ⓑ Ⓒ Ⓓ

## Part 1 Photographs

*You'll see a picture and hear four short statements. Choose the statement that best describes what you see in the picture.*

**1**

Ⓐ Ⓑ Ⓒ Ⓓ

**2**

Ⓐ Ⓑ Ⓒ Ⓓ

# Part 2 Question - Response  ((·))2-77,78,79,80

*You'll hear a question followed by three responses. Choose the best response to each question.*

3. Mark your answer on your answer sheet.  Ⓐ Ⓑ Ⓒ

4. Mark your answer on your answer sheet.  Ⓐ Ⓑ Ⓒ

5. Mark your answer on your answer sheet.  Ⓐ Ⓑ Ⓒ

6. Mark your answer on your answer sheet.  Ⓐ Ⓑ Ⓒ


# Part 3 Conversation  ((·))2-81,82

*You'll hear one conversation between two people and read three questions followed by four answers. Choose the best answer to each question.*

7. Who most likely is management negotiating with?
   (A) A government agency
   (B) An individual employee
   (C) A rival company
   (D) A labor union

   Ⓐ Ⓑ Ⓒ Ⓓ


8. What have they already agreed on?
   (A) A pension plan
   (B) Overtime pay
   (C) Health benefits
   (D) Unemployment insurance

   Ⓐ Ⓑ Ⓒ Ⓓ


9. Why does the man say, "Good question"?
   (A) He is happy to answer the woman's question.
   (B) He cannot answer the woman's question.
   (C) He wants to use this question at the next negotiation.
   (D) He is surprised by the woman's question.

   Ⓐ Ⓑ Ⓒ Ⓓ

## Part 4 Talk 2-83,84

*You'll hear one talk and read three questions about the talk. The questions will be followed by four answers. Choose the best answer to each question.*

10. How often is this meeting held?
    (A) Once a week
    (B) Once a month
    (C) Once every three months
    (D) Once a year

    Ⓐ Ⓑ Ⓒ Ⓓ

11. Who is most likely the speaker?
    (A) A personnel manager
    (B) A sales manager
    (C) A shareholder
    (D) A secretary

    Ⓐ Ⓑ Ⓒ Ⓓ

12. What is one thing this company would like to do next year?
    (A) Close some branches
    (B) Raise prices
    (C) Sell more products
    (D) Develop new markets overseas

    Ⓐ Ⓑ Ⓒ Ⓓ

---

### TOEIC 攻略のコツ：[新形式] Part 7
### インスタントメッセージ（チャット）問題の対策

Part 7のインスタントメッセージ(チャット)問題では、名前と時間が入った（例：Hathaway David [8:54 A.M.]）短いメッセージが時間順に並べられ、他の読解問題と異なり会話形式のくだけた文章を特徴としています。Sure thing（いいとも）、Absolutely（全くその通り）、Too bad（お気の毒に）などがその例です。このような問題では、人間関係やチャットの目的などの状況把握がとくに重要になります。また、設問に時間や名前が明記されていることが多いので、これを頼りに scanning でヒントを探して解答しましょう。

136

# ■ Reading

## 文法問題攻略のポイント：条件文など

1. 命令・要求・必要などを表す述語に続く that 節中には動詞の原形が用いられる。（仮定法現在）

　　例1：<u>I insisted that</u> he **visit** the customer again to negotiate with him.

　　例2：<u>It is important that</u> you **make** contact with your clients regularly.

2. 現在の事実と反対の仮定には過去形が用いられる。（仮定法過去）

　　例：<u>If I</u> **had** any spare time, I <u>could complete</u> all these documents.

3. 過去の事実と反対の仮定には過去完了形が用いられる。（仮定法過去完了）

　　例：<u>If we</u> **had acquired** U & AI Enterprise sooner, it <u>would</u> not <u>have gone</u> bankrupt.

4. 仮定法を用いるその他の表現

　　例：<u>I wish</u> I **had** not **bought** so many stocks.

## Part 5 Incomplete Sentences

*A word or phrase is missing in each sentence. Choose the best answer to complete the sentence.*

13. I suggest that you _____ the scanner to send a copy of the contract.
 (A) use
 (B) used
 (C) had used
 (D) would use

Ⓐ Ⓑ Ⓒ Ⓓ

14. Unless we _____ an invitation to Bill, he will not come to our sales meeting.
 (A) did not send
 (B) sent
 (C) send
 (D) had not sent

Ⓐ Ⓑ Ⓒ Ⓓ

15. We would definitely do business with those customers if only they _____ clear leadership in promoting the industry.
 (A) shown
 (B) showed
 (C) will have shown
 (D) are showing

Ⓐ Ⓑ Ⓒ Ⓓ

16. _____ Jennifer's assistance, we could never have succeeded in concluding a contract with ACM Trading.
 (A) With
 (B) Without
 (C) But
 (D) Had it not been

Ⓐ Ⓑ Ⓒ Ⓓ

# Part 6 Text Completion

*Read the following text. A word, phrase, or sentence is missing. Choose the best answer to complete the text.*

*Questions 17-19 refer to the following letter.*

Helen Schelader
Office Manager
SilverWay Holdings Co. Ltd.
171 Orange St. Seattle
WA98202

Dear Mr. Pierre Dubois,
With regard to the proposal you have presented, I would like to meet with you sometime in December to discuss ways (    17    ) which we might be able to cooperate. (    18    ) if you would get in touch with my secretary Kim Robinson to (    19    ) a meeting at a mutually convenient time and place.

With best wishes,
*Helen Schelader*
Helen Schelader

17. (A) of
    (B) to
    (C) in
    (D) at

Ⓐ Ⓑ Ⓒ Ⓓ

18. (A) Please let me know
    (B) I'm not sure
    (C) I would appreciate it very much
    (D) I would be available

Ⓐ Ⓑ Ⓒ Ⓓ

19. (A) put up
    (B) set up
    (C) make up
    (D) take up

Ⓐ Ⓑ Ⓒ Ⓓ

# Part 7 Reading Comprehension

*Read the following texts. Each text or set of texts is followed by several questions. Choose the best answer to each question.*

*Questions 20-22 refer to the following e-mail.*

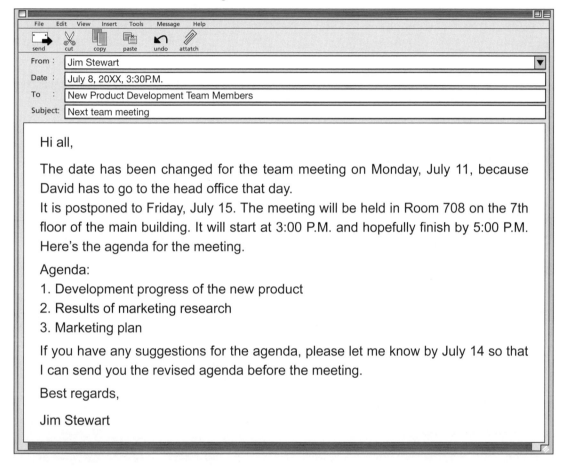

From: Jim Stewart
Date: July 8, 20XX, 3:30 P.M.
To: New Product Development Team Members
Subject: Next team meeting

Hi all,

The date has been changed for the team meeting on Monday, July 11, because David has to go to the head office that day.

It is postponed to Friday, July 15. The meeting will be held in Room 708 on the 7th floor of the main building. It will start at 3:00 P.M. and hopefully finish by 5:00 P.M. Here's the agenda for the meeting.

Agenda:
1. Development progress of the new product
2. Results of marketing research
3. Marketing plan

If you have any suggestions for the agenda, please let me know by July 14 so that I can send you the revised agenda before the meeting.

Best regards,

Jim Stewart

20. Why is the meeting postponed?
   (A) Someone in the team will not be available.
   (B) They need more time to prepare documents.
   (C) Their product development is behind schedule.
   (D) There will be a visitor from the head office.

21. When will the meeting be held?
   (A) On July 8
   (B) On July 11
   (C) On July 14
   (D) On July 15

22. What will be discussed in the meeting?
   (A) The introduction of the new director of the development team
   (B) The market situation of the new product
   (C) The budget for the new product development
   (D) A complaint about the new product from a customer

Questions 23-24 refer to the following e-mail.

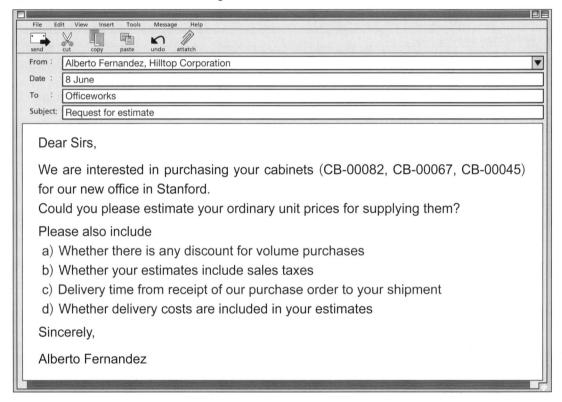

23. Why is Alberto Fernandez sending an email to Officeworks?
   (A) To remind Officeworks to ship the cabinets he ordered
   (B) To ask Officeworks to send him a catalogue of cabinets
   (C) To ask Officeworks to let him know prices of some cabinets
   (D) To ask Officeworks to deliver the cabinets he ordered

24. What does Alberto Fernandez want to know?
   (A) Whether there is a warranty for the cabinets
   (B) How the payment for the cabinets should be made
   (C) How long it will take to ship the cabinets
   (D) How many cabinets are in stock

· · · · · · · · · · · · · · · · · ·

## **E**xpand your vocabulary! ―イディオムに強くなろう！⑶

➤ **at a loss**「途方にくれて」
➤ **be aware of**「～に気づいて」
➤ **break out**「起こる」
➤ **can afford to**「～する余裕がある」
➤ **catch up**「追いつく・遅れを取り戻す」
➤ **due to / because of / on account of**「（理由・原因）のために」

➤ **fill in**［out］「記入する」
➤ **fill up**「満たす・満タンにする」
➤ **on board**「搭乗して」
➤ **on behalf of**「～を代表して」

## **L**earn more! ― **V**ocabulary in **C**ontext

*Complete each English sentence according to its Japanese translation. The first letter is given.*

1. We do not seem to be (m              ) any (p              ) now. How about putting this problem on hold for now?

   （今は進展しそうもありませんから、とりあえずこの問題は保留しておいてはどうでしょうか？）

2. The market is advancing now; therefore, we cannot possibly (g              ) that we will be able to offer this price when our (p              )(s              ) is exhausted.

   （相場は今上昇しています。そこで現在の在庫がなくなれば、この値段と同じ値段でご提供するということは、とうてい保証することはできなくなります。）

3. Under special agreements with a (l              )(m              ), we offer you competitive prices for quality electronic products.

   （トップメーカーとの特約により、我が社は他社に負けない価格で高品質の電子製品をご提供させていただいております。）

4. You say that we couldn't get our client to (a              )(t              ) these conditions. But you'll never know unless you try.

   （お客様をこの条件に同意するよう説得することができないと言いますが、やってみないとわかりませんよ。）

---

1. making, progress 2. guarantee, present, stock 3. leading manufacturer 4. agree to

# SCOREBOARD (Photocopiable)

Class: ☐　　No: ☐　　Name: ☐

17／24（70％）以上取れるように頑張りましょう。
L：Listening　R：Reading　T：Total
（Part I〜IVの得点と寸評を記入し、折れ線グラフを描きましょう）

| Unit | 1 | | | 2 | | | 3 | | | 4 | | | 5 | | |
|---|---|---|---|---|---|---|---|---|---|---|---|---|---|---|---|
| Score | L | R | T | L | R | T | L | R | T | L | R | T | L | R | T |
| | /12 | /12 | /24 | /12 | /12 | /24 | /12 | /12 | /24 | /12 | /12 | /24 | /12 | /12 | /24 |
| Student's Comments | | | | | | | | | | | | | | | |
| Teacher's Comments | | | | | | | | | | | | | | | |
| Unit | 6 | | | 7 | | | 8 | | | 9 | | | 10 | | |
| Score | L | R | T | L | R | T | L | R | T | L | R | T | L | R | T |
| | /12 | /12 | /24 | /12 | /12 | /24 | /12 | /12 | /24 | /12 | /12 | /24 | /12 | /12 | /24 |
| Student's Comments | | | | | | | | | | | | | | | |
| Teacher's Comments | | | | | | | | | | | | | | | |
| Unit | 11 | | | 12 | | | 13 | | | 14 | | | 15 | | |
| Score | L | R | T | L | R | T | L | R | T | L | R | T | L | R | T |
| | /12 | /12 | /24 | /12 | /12 | /24 | /12 | /12 | /24 | /12 | /12 | /24 | /12 | /12 | /24 |
| Student's Comments | | | | | | | | | | | | | | | |
| Teacher's Comments | | | | | | | | | | | | | | | |

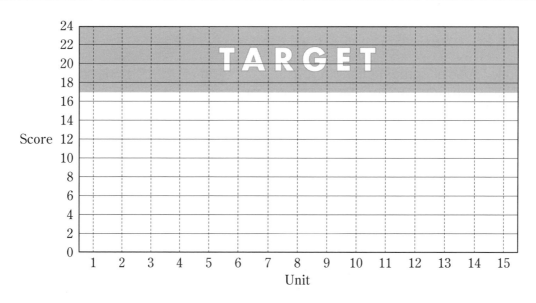

# Vocabulary List

| 単語 | Page | | 単語 | Page |
|------|------|---|------|------|
| ☐ abide by | 6 | | ☐ attitude | 96 |
| ☐ aboard | 15 | | ☐ audience | 6 |
| ☐ accelerate | 69 | | ☐ bachelor | 78 |
| ☐ accomadation | 41 | | ☐ balance | 105 |
| ☐ accountant | 78 | | ☐ bet | 51 |
| ☐ accurate | 68 | | ☐ beverage | 33 |
| ☐ accustomed | 6 | | ☐ biological | 60 |
| ☐ achieve | 115 | | ☐ boarding pass | 33 |
| ☐ acquire | 133 | | ☐ book | 33 |
| ☐ adopt | 68,87 | | ☐ brochure | 33 |
| ☐ affect | 60 | | ☐ budget | 105 |
| ☐ agency | 87 | | ☐ buffet | 15 |
| ☐ agenda | 133 | | ☐ burden | 60 |
| ☐ agree to | 141 | | ☐ cancer | 24 |
| ☐ alergic | 32 | | ☐ care for | 15 |
| ☐ alternate | 78 | | ☐ cargo | 50 |
| ☐ alternative | 69 | | ☐ characteristic | 69 |
| ☐ ambitious | 78 | | ☐ checkup | 24 |
| ☐ amusement park | 6 | | ☐ chemical | 60 |
| ☐ analyze | 60 | | ☐ clap | 14 |
| ☐ annual | 24 | | ☐ classified | 87 |
| ☐ apologize | 33 | | ☐ colleague | 15 |
| ☐ appetite | 23 | | ☐ comfort | 115 |
| ☐ appetizer | 23 | | ☐ commission | 42 |
| ☐ applaude | 6 | | ☐ commitment | 51 |
| ☐ applicance | 51 | | ☐ commodity | 87 |
| ☐ applicant | 87 | | ☐ commuter | 33 |
| ☐ appointment | 96 | | ☐ compliant | 60 |
| ☐ appreciate | 51 | | ☐ component | 24,59 |
| ☐ approve of | 115 | | ☐ composer | 14 |
| ☐ architect | 33 | | ☐ condominium | 124 |
| ☐ assembly | 51 | | ☐ conduct | 24 |
| ☐ astronomy | 33 | | ☐ conference | 115 |
| ☐ attachment | 96 | | ☐ confidential | 60 |

| | | | | | |
|---|---|---|---|---|---|
| ☐ crowded | 41 | | ☐ donate | 105 |
| ☐ connect | 96 | | ☐ dormitory | 124 |
| ☐ construction | 124 | | ☐ durable | 51 |
| ☐ contract | 51 | | ☐ durable | 59 |
| ☐ contractor | 59 | | ☐ efficient | 51 |
| ☐ convenience | 95 | | ☐ elcetromagnet | 69 |
| ☐ cooperate | 133 | | ☐ emit | 69 |
| ☐ copper | 69 | | ☐ enable | 42 |
| ☐ costume | 6 | | ☐ encourage | 115 |
| ☐ cottage | 124 | | ☐ enthusiastic | 87 |
| ☐ counselor | 24 | | ☐ environment | 69 |
| ☐ countryside | 124 | | ☐ environmentaly friendly | 51 |
| ☐ courier | 33 | | ☐ era | 69 |
| ☐ crash | 69 | | ☐ eventually | 24 |
| ☐ crew | 15 | | ☐ excluding | 42 |
| ☐ critic | 14 | | ☐ exhaust | 69 |
| ☐ currency | 105 | | ☐ exhibit | 6 |
| ☐ customs | 42 | | ☐ expire | 42 |
| ☐ cutback | 59 | | ☐ explore | 24,60 |
| ☐ deadline | 24 | | ☐ extension | 96 |
| ☐ defect | 51 | | ☐ extension number | 96 |
| ☐ delay | 33 | | ☐ fabulous | 15 |
| ☐ departure | 33 | | ☐ facility | 24 |
| ☐ deposit | 105 | | ☐ factor | 24 |
| ☐ description | 78 | | ☐ fare | 33 |
| ☐ deserve | 133 | | ☐ farewell | 78 |
| ☐ destination | 42 | | ☐ feature | 24 |
| ☐ device | 87 | | ☐ fee | 6 |
| ☐ diner | 15 | | ☐ finance | 105 |
| ☐ director | 14 | | ☐ financial integration | 114 |
| ☐ disappointed | 14 | | ☐ financial report | 105 |
| ☐ discourage | 6 | | ☐ fit in with | 77 |
| ☐ diseases | 24 | | ☐ for free | 15 |
| ☐ dismiss | 133 | | ☐ fossil fuel | 51 |
| ☐ dissolve | 15 | | ☐ freight | 42 |
| ☐ distributor | 50 | | ☐ frequent | 33 |
| ☐ document | 115 | | ☐ fuel | 51 |

| | | | | | |
|---|---|---|---|---|---|
| ☐ fully equipped | 132 | | ☐ laboratory | 60 |
| ☐ genetic | 60 | | ☐ landlord | 124 |
| ☐ goal | 133 | | ☐ landscape | 6 |
| ☐ graduate | 6 | | ☐ leading manufacturer | 141 |
| ☐ grand total | 42 | | ☐ leisurely | 6 |
| ☐ gratitude | 23 | | ☐ levitation | 69 |
| ☐ guarantee | 96 | | ☐ lifetime employment | 87 |
| ☐ guideway | 69 | | ☐ local call | 104 |
| ☐ heart attack | 24 | | ☐ local town | 132 |
| ☐ hold on | 104 | | ☐ long distance call | 104 |
| ☐ hold one's breath | 14 | | ☐ look over | 104 |
| ☐ hospitality | 23 | | ☐ luncheon | 15 |
| ☐ household | 59 | | ☐ luxury | 41 |
| ☐ humidity | 51 | | ☐ maintain | 115 |
| ☐ hung up | 96 | | ☐ make an appointment | 96 |
| ☐ hypothesis | 60 | | ☐ make delivery | 42 |
| ☐ impact | 24 | | ☐ make sure to | 114 |
| ☐ imply | 68 | | ☐ market share | 133 |
| ☐ in advance | 123 | | ☐ mash | 15 |
| ☐ in charge of | 115 | | ☐ massive | 87 |
| ☐ in detail | 95 | | ☐ mechanical | 87 |
| ☐ ingredient | 15 | | ☐ medical insurance | 32 |
| ☐ inquire | 42 | | ☐ meet standards | 115 |
| ☐ inspection | 96,115 | | ☐ meet demand | 68 |
| ☐ install | 6 | | ☐ minimal | 96 |
| ☐ intake | 15 | | ☐ mobile | 96 |
| ☐ integration | 114 | | ☐ mobility | 51 |
| ☐ internal | 115 | | ☐ moderate | 15 |
| ☐ interpersonal | 87 | | ☐ monthly | 96 |
| ☐ intersection | 33 | | ☐ musical instrument | 6 |
| ☐ invest | 105 | | ☐ mutually | 133 |
| ☐ investigate | 60 | | ☐ navigate | 51 |
| ☐ invoice | 133 | | ☐ negotiate | 133 |
| ☐ involve | 60 | | ☐ neighborhood | 124 |
| ☐ itinerary | 33 | | ☐ nominate | 6 |
| ☐ keep in good shape | 24 | | ☐ novel | 14 |
| ☐ labor shortage | 87 | | ☐ nuisance | 69 |

| | | | | |
|---|---|---|---|---|
| ☐ nutrition | 24 | | ☐ raw material | 51 |
| ☐ observation | 68 | | ☐ real estate | 124 |
| ☐ obstacle | 51 | | ☐ recession | 105 |
| ☐ obtain | 42 | | ☐ recharge | 96 |
| ☐ obvious | 68 | | ☐ recipe | 15 |
| ☐ opportunity | 78 | | ☐ recommendation | 60 |
| ☐ output | 59 | | ☐ recover from | 24 |
| ☐ patience | 42 | | ☐ recruit | 87 |
| ☐ patron | 15 | | ☐ reduce | 105 |
| ☐ pedestrian | 33 | | ☐ refer to | 114 |
| ☐ pension | 105 | | ☐ reference | 86 |
| ☐ personal information | 123 | | ☐ refrain from | 23 |
| ☐ place an order | 42 | | ☐ refund | 41 |
| ☐ poll | 60 | | ☐ region | 124 |
| ☐ postage | 96 | | ☐ register | 78 |
| ☐ postpone | 41 | | ☐ registered | 78 |
| ☐ prediction | 133 | | ☐ reject | 115 |
| ☐ prescription | 32 | | ☐ renenerative | 69 |
| ☐ preserve | 69 | | ☐ renewable | 86 |
| ☐ procedure | 60 | | ☐ rent | 124 |
| ☐ profit | 133 | | ☐ repel | 69 |
| ☐ prohibit | 6 | | ☐ replace | 115 |
| ☐ promote | 78 | | ☐ replacement | 95 |
| ☐ promotional | 87 | | ☐ representative | 78 |
| ☐ promptly | 42 | | ☐ reputation | 6,114 |
| ☐ property | 124 | | ☐ requirement | 87 |
| ☐ proposal | 115 | | ☐ resignation | 78 |
| ☐ public relations | 87 | | ☐ restiriction | 42 |
| ☐ publish | 133 | | ☐ résumé | 78 |
| ☐ purse | 33 | | ☐ revenue | 133 |
| ☐ pursue | 133 | | ☐ revise | 115 |
| ☐ put through | 96 | | ☐ reward | 78 |
| ☐ put together | 59 | | ☐ ripe | 15 |
| ☐ qualification | 87 | | ☐ rural | 124 |
| ☐ quality control | 51 | | ☐ savings accout | 105 |
| ☐ quote | 124 | | ☐ sculpture | 6 |
| ☐ raise awareness | 24 | | ☐ second-hand | 115 |

| | | | | |
|---|---|---|---|---|
| ☐ settle | 133 | ☐ temporary worker] | 123 |
| ☐ shareholder | 133 | ☐ text | 96 |
| ☐ shipping charge | 42 | ☐ thermal | 115 |
| ☐ side effect | 32 | ☐ thrilling | 6 |
| ☐ sign up for | 86 | ☐ tracking number | 42 |
| ☐ sociable | 78 | ☐ transaction | 105 |
| ☐ solution | 68 | ☐ transfer | 105 |
| ☐ souvenir | 33 | ☐ transportation | 50 |
| ☐ spam | 96 | ☐ treatment | 32 |
| ☐ special effect | 6 | ☐ under review | 86 |
| ☐ status | 42 | ☐ undergo | 115 |
| ☐ stock investment | 105 | ☐ unemployment rate | 78 |
| ☐ stop over | 33 | ☐ upgrade | 69 |
| ☐ subcontractor | 59 | ☐ urban | 124 |
| ☐ submit | 78 | ☐ utitilites | 132 |
| ☐ substance | 60 | ☐ vacancy | 87 |
| ☐ suffer from | 24 | ☐ vessle | 50 |
| ☐ suggestion | 133 | ☐ via | 42 |
| ☐ suitable for | 77 | ☐ virus | 96 |
| ☐ surplus | 115 | ☐ vulnerable | 105 |
| ☐ sustainable | 124 | ☐ warranty | 42 |
| ☐ sustainable development | 124 | ☐ withdraw | 105 |
| ☐ symptom | 32 | ☐ worthwhile | 6 |
| ☐ teller | 105 | ☐ wrong number | 96 |

## TEXT PRODUCTION STAFF

| edited by | 編集 |
|---|---|
| Hiroko Nakazawa | 中澤ひろ子 |

| English-language editing by | 英文校閲 |
|---|---|
| Bill Benfield | ビル・ベンフィールド |

| cover design by | 表紙デザイン |
|---|---|
| Ruben Frosali | ルーベン・フロサリ |

## CD PRODUCTION STAFF

| recorded by | 吹き込み者 |
|---|---|
| Jack Merluzzi (AmE) | ジャック・マルージー（アメリカ英語） |
| Carolyn Miller (CnE) | キャロリン・ミラー（カナダ英語） |
| Nadia Mckechnie (BrE) | ナディア・マクックニー（イギリス英語） |
| Brad Holms (AsE) | ブラッド・ホームズ（オーストラリア英語） |
| Howard Colefield (AmE) | ハワード・コルフィールド（アメリカ英語） |
| Andree Dufleit (CnE) | アンドレ・デュフレ（カナダ英語） |
| Emma Howard (BrE) | エマ・ハワード（イギリス英語） |

# ESSENTIAL APPROACH FOR THE TOEIC® L&R TEST
## ―Revised Edition―
## TOEIC® L&R TESTへのニューアプローチ　―改訂版―

2019年 1 月20日　初 版 発 行
2025年 2 月20日　第 7 刷 発 行

著　者　大須賀 直子　塚野 壽一　山本 厚子
　　　　Robert Van Benthuysen

発行者　佐野 英一郎

発行所　株式会社 成 美 堂
　　　　〒101-0052東京都千代田区神田小川町3-22
　　　　TEL 03-3291-2261　　　FAX 03-3293-5490
　　　　http://www.seibido.co.jp

印刷・製本　倉敷印刷株式会社

ISBN 978-4-7919-7189-3　　　　　　　　　　　Printed in Japan

・落丁・乱丁本はお取り替えします。
・本書の無断複写は、著作権上の例外を除き著作権侵害となります。